The Mythology of Mesopotamia

Fascinating Insights, Myths, Stories & History From The World's Most Ancient Civilization. Sumerian, Akkadian, Babylonian, Persian, Assyrian, and More

History Brought Alive

—

from various sources. Please consult a licensed professional before attempting any techniques outlined in this book.

By reading this document, the reader agrees that under no circumstances is the author responsible for any losses, direct or indirect, that are incurred as a result of the use of the information contained within this document, including, but not limited to, errors, omissions, or inaccuracies.

Free Bonus from HBA: Ebook Bundle

Greetings!

First of all, thank you for reading our books. As fellow passionate readers of history and mythology we aim to create the very best books for our readers.

Now, we invite you to join our VIP list. As a welcome gift we offer the History & Mythology Ebook Bundle below for free. Plus you can be the first to receive new books and exclusives! Remember it's 100% free to join.

Simply follow the link below to join.

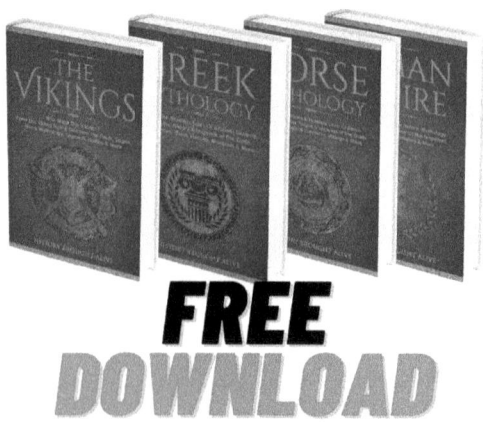

(https://www.subscribepage.com/hba)

Keep upto date with us on:

YouTube: History Brought Alive

Facebook: History Brought Alive

www.historybroughtalive.com

Table of Contents

—

References 158

Introduction

We go through our lives with an overall sense of permanence. Perhaps it is due to our living only a short span in a world which, while ever-changing, continues to function around the same basic principles of society and culture. Life is, for the most part, relatively predictable. Human society seems like a constant, even if it changes shape from time to time. Our ability to think, to dream, to build, and to create, is so deeply ingrained into the human psyche that we feel they must always have been there. Genuinely comprehending a time when we were incapable of these things is difficult.

But it was not always so. We were not always the builders of great civilizations, the creators of art and war. There was a time when our grandest congregations were merely small villages, and times before that when we wandered from place to place, living off the land, not unlike all other animals. Everything has a beginning, and everything that occurs has a *cause*, a reason for its genesis. When it comes to civilization, the reasons are many, and they are uncertain. But there is one key similarity between each of the early Eurasian civilizations, which sprung up independently of one another, spread across the globe.

Across Europe and Asia were four of the "cradles of civilization," and each of these four was built along a river. On the banks of the Nile, the great civilization of Egypt rose, dominating the Mediterranean until Alexander's conquests several thousand years later. In the mid-lower basin of the Yellow River, the earliest Chinese civilization rose to regional prominence. Along the Indus, in modern-day Pakistan, the mysterious Indus Valley civilization emerged. But perhaps most significant of all early civilizations was that whose foundations were laid in the fertile lands between the Euphrates and the Tigris in modern-day Iraq and Syria—the Mesopotamians.

The term 'Mesopotamian' is made up of the ancient term *meso* meaning between, and the word *potamos* meaning river, literally translating to "between the rivers." As in Egypt, China, and Pakistan, it was these rivers and the fertile valley which lay between them that allowed the civilization to progress first from Palaeolithic hunter-gatherer societies to an agricultural, village community, and finally through the urban revolution and into a city-dwelling culture. This transition from farm to city was perhaps one of the most significant changes in human history, surpassed only by that from hunter-gatherer to agricultural community coming before it. While this occurred across Eurasia and even in Mesoamerica and Peru around similar periods, what makes Mesopotamia particularly interesting is the fact that it happened there first. As such, despite the independent rise of cities in other areas, Mesopotamia represents the true origins of what we now call 'civilization,' and it is this fact that makes it enormously significant to the narrative of human history.

Mesopotamia is also interesting for many other reasons. First is the creativity of the era—cuneiform writing, the wheel, and an enormous list of other creations over their extraordinarily long period of dominance in writing, construction, science, law, literature and poetry, music, and the building of empires. They have given us an immense number of global 'firsts': the first schools, historians, lullabies, legal precedents, pharmacopeias, aquariums, libraries and library catalogues, the first almanacs, the first animal fables, and the first literary debates. From Mesopotamian culture we inherited the love song, paid employment, moral idealism, tax reductions, bicameral governments, tales of apocalyptic floods and resurrections, and even the first cases of juvenile delinquency. They provided the entire framework for modern civilization. Without their contributions, we could have never reached the social, political, cultural, and technological heights of today.

Another area of interest is the lack of any dominant ethnicity. Mesopotamian civilization, made up of several major empires, numerous cities, spread across an extended period of history, was not merely made up of a local dominant race but of hundreds of different groups of people—immigrants and outsiders were no less significant than the Semitic and non-Semitic locals, and many even rose to prominent positions of power or even kingship. The civilization grew and continued over thousands of years, while the ethnicity of those running and living within it was varied and changing.

Lastly, there is the incredible longevity of the Mesopotamian civilization. From the invention of cuneiform around 3,000 BCE to the conquest of Babylon by Cyrus the Great of Persia in 539 BCE, the independent Mesopotamia lasted somewhere around 2,500 years. If you take the beginning not from the invention of writing but instead from the founding of Uruk around 4,500 BCE, that number increases to 4,000 years. For context—there were around 2,500 years between the conquests of Cyrus and the modern-day. The independent Mesopotamian civilization ruled the area for upward of half of human history. During this time, empires rose and fell, certain cities or regions within Mesopotamia gained dominance and lost it, but the civilization itself stood strong. In fact, not only was the region independent for such a long period but its culture was also preserved remarkably well. Languages, music, writing systems, scientific and religious traditions were maintained throughout the civilization for its duration, and while changes will have occurred with time, they remained recognizable and understandable from the beginning until the very end.

Mesopotamia, while fascinating, is poorly represented in popular history, dwarfed by Rome or Classical Greece, or even Egypt. For a long time, the only way to understand Mesopotamian history, culture, and mythology has been through dense, academic, or semi-academic sources. This is in part due to the huge time frame, the rise and fall of various empires, and the lack of easily understood ancient sources. The inaccessibility of information about this remarkable civilization means that many people know little about it, and what they do know may be skewed in the direction of pseudo-history and alien-overlord conspiracy theories, derived from very specific interpretations of ancient mythological sources. As such, it is essential to bring the knowledge and history of Mesopotamia into the light, making it accessible to all, allowing everyone to benefit from the fascinating insight of the very first human civilization.

In this book, we will be discussing the history of Mesopotamia from the urbanization and the rise of Uruk to the fall of Babylon to the Persians in 539 BCE. We will delve into the Sumerians, the Akkadians, the Assyrian Empire, and the Babylonians, discussing their culture, technology, leadership; their art and their war, their rise, and their fall. We will then take a look at some of the Mesopotamian epics and mythological stories, including the famous *Epic of Gilgamesh* and the Babylonian creation myth, the *Enuma Elish*. Through careful, accurate examination of both archaeological sources and the academic work of expert historians, the tales of Ancient Mesopotamia will be carried forth from the fog of time. For too long now, information on this fascinating period has been too sparse, too dense, inaccessible. It is time for the history of Mesopotamia to be brought alive.

Part 1:

The History

Chapter 1: Kingship Descends From Heaven (ca. 5400-2350 BCE)

Temple Rule

It is important to remember that Sumer was not an empire, nor even a nation, but simply a civilization—a collection of cultural practices, social attitudes, rituals, beliefs, and technology shared between a group of people. Technically speaking, civilization is usually underlined by a writing system and record-keeping, the cultural developments associated with the written word. That said, to understand the rise of Mesopotamia we must delve back beyond the advent of cuneiform, the alphabet used to write Sumerian and other local languages, and explore instead a period prior.

The early cities of southern Mesopotamia first emerged in the fifth millennium BCE, with Eridu, the city of the god Enki, being founded sometime around the year 5000 BCE, followed around 500 years later by the city of Gilgamesh,

Uruk. While it is uncertain how the cities were founded, it is likely that the move from agricultural villages to city life evolved around the foundation of religion or belief—this is evident in the early city structure of Sumer, where rather than a monarchy, the first cities were instead defined by temple rule. It is suggested that the early cities of Mesopotamia were founded in locations of regular congregation. In the agricultural era of human history, there would have been times when migration to certain areas was beneficial or even necessary due to plentiful food or fertile ground. People would gather in such areas and, at some point, may have left a monument of sorts in a solid, permanent material, such as baked-clay bricks, a sharp contrast to the typical, temporary huts. This anchor for humanity would stand for generations and may have encouraged others to come and see it. Archaeological evidence suggests that within, and beneath, the immense temples of the Sumerian cities lay the foundations of progressively smaller structures. In a sense, the city radiated out from this central point, as did civilization itself.

The rise of Eridu was followed shortly by the rise of Uruk. According to Sumerian mythology, the god Enki ruled Eridu yet kept the *Me* (pronounced *Meh*, a difficult word to translate, but meaning something similar to divine decrees for culture and the basis of civilization), hidden, only for use by him and in his city. His daughter, Inanna, another god, stole the *Me* from Enki and brought them to her own city of Uruk, thus spreading civilization to her people. Sometimes referred to as the first 'true' city, Uruk was the location of several huge advancements in human society.

By far the most important invention of Uruk, however, was writing. Beginning with logographic symbols many years prior and being used to record simple bureaucratic and administrative notes such as payments of grain, the first full writing system was in use by around the year 3200 BCE. It was around this time that, according to the traditional definition, 'civilization' truly began.

The invention of writing was of extreme importance to Uruk and Sumer as a whole. Not only did it make the recording of administrative notes much easier, but it also developed the sense of personal identity in the city, something that went on to have immense effects on the future of Sumer as a whole and contributed to the transition from temple rule to kingship. Archeologists have uncovered numerous cylindrical seals, or *kishib*, from around this period which were used for signing documents or for labeling personal property. The *kishib* represented an immense change in the ideology of the people of Sumer, as it became a symbol of personal identity and branding. The importance of the individual was, before this point, overshadowed by that of the community. The prevalent use of the *kishib*, however, demonstrated the newfound importance of the individual within the collective community. It is this, in part, that would lead to a dramatic restructuring of Sumerian society as a whole.

The Flood

The Bible tells us of Noah and the apocalyptic flood sent by the Hebrew God to wipe most of humanity from the planet. While some take this as fact and others consider it biblical fiction or a metaphor, it is not merely the Bible that tells this story of an apocalyptic flood.

Floods, both in the past and in the future, are common in mythology. The obvious is Yahweh's Flood in *Genesis*, but in the Hindu texts *Satapatha Brahmana* and *Puranas*, Vishnu warns the first man of an impending flood and asks him to build a boat; in the Gun-Yu myth of ancient China, an enormous flood occurs which lasts two generations; even Plato describes a flood-myth in his dialogue *Timaeus*, where Prometheus tells Deucalion to build an ark in preparation for Zeus' incoming flood. Norse, Polynesian, Irish, and Mayan mythology, among others, also tell of floods. But the Mesopotamian tale of the Flood, as told in the *Epic of Gilgamesh* and the Akkadian *Atrahasis*, is perhaps the earliest Flood story that we know of.

The *Gilgamesh* version of the Flood story is the one closest to that in the *Book of Genesis*, and of the versions of the epic, it is the 700 BCE Babylonian copy that appears most similar. Considering that *Genesis* was believed to be written at a similar time, it may have been influenced by the Babylonian *Gilgamesh*, which in turn appears to have drawn from the Akkadian *Atrahasis* from the 18th century BCE. Regardless of the edition, however, it is hard to date the Flood to a certain period in history, though it is most certainly a long time before the tales were written. That said, at some point around the year 3000 BCE, the social and political structure of Mesopotamia changed dramatically, and it is believed by many that "the Flood" is less a historical deluge and more a metaphorical representation of dramatic societal change.

Historian Paul Kriwaczek (2010) suggests that "the Flood" may be representative, at least in part, of the change in the Urukian society and also the fall of temple rule. As discussed, the people of Sumer and Uruk, in particular, were moving away from the basic, collective social structure they had developed, one that was headed by the rule of priests in central temples. Theocracies rarely last long before being supplanted by more pragmatic forms of governance, and it is unsurprising that as Sumerian society developed, it outgrew its original leadership.

The soil around Uruk was rich in minerals and salt, in part due to the nature of the two rivers. This was not necessarily a good thing and could prove disastrous regarding irrigation. Over the centuries, the people of Sumer learned to deal with the problems posed by the mineral-rich water by leaving the fields fallow, allowing the soil time to recover. As such, the fields would generally produce crops every two years, and with a growing population, this may not have been seen as enough. It is not hard to imagine priests and religious figures, ruling the city from their temples and knowing little of the farming life, ordering the people not to leave the soil fallow as they had done, and thus (in theory) producing twice the resources. It would have been an inevitable disaster; according to the *Atrahasis*, "the black fields became white, the broad plain was choked with salt" (Kriwaczek, 2010).

Civilizations structured around an ideology or belief, and figure-headed by a representation of that belief (as is seen in temple-rule society) are easily toppled in periods of instability. It is not difficult for an ideology to prove incorrect, and when that illusion has been shattered, there is little one can do to repair it. A disaster such as this, bringing with it disease, famine, and death, would prove the end of temple rule, destroying the ideology that had sustained it.

While supreme god Enlil and Hebrew God Yahweh may have had differing motives in their respective tales, the floods they brought were an attempt to wipe humanity from the planet. They represented a dramatic change in the social order, to the point where the history of such civilizations can be divided into pre- and post-deluge eras. Mythology and ancient history are rarely literal—whether there was a genuine flood or not, the deluge is used as a representation of widespread change. Brought about in part by the advent of writing, in part by famine or disease, and most certainly by the faltering of ideology, "the Flood" became a convenient symbol separating the old Sumer from the new. The old was rejected, faith faltered, and the Urukian period of domination was coming to an end. The *Sumerian King List* puts this quite simply at the end of the first section, a hard line dividing the old period from the new: "Then the Flood swept over" (Livius.org, 2020).

A New Order

It is from ruins that great things arise. It has been this way for millennia—change, new orders, need not only a reason to form but a space to form within. When things are working well, people adopt a conservative attitude toward life and toward change. When things are falling apart, it is the progressive attitude that wins out, the creativity of those who seek to cast down the failing relics of times before and instead erect a grand new experiment, something designed to, theoretically, overcome the flaws of the past. So, like the proverbial phoenix rising from the ashes of temple rule, a new form of leadership and governance came into being across the lands of Sumer.

This was by no means an immediate change. Even the best ideas need time to grow organically, to flesh themselves out, and to reach their full potential. Kingship in Sumer was not bestowed overnight. Instead, in the power gap left by the diminishing temples, new men stepped forward, and those new men slowly but surely consolidated power in their cities.

It began, as so many major historical events do, with a change in Sumerian socioeconomic structure, although this term may suggest a more complex system than what they had in place at the time. Ultimately, the growing importance of the individual within society had led to the emergence of a new class structure, one that would lay the foundations for millennia to come—and the entire process began with barley.

Barley is a good crop for areas with high levels of salt and minerals in the soil. As discussed above, the land between the Tigris and the Euphrates had high levels of salinity, and the disastrous effects of poor crop management may have led to this becoming an even more pressing issue. As such, the regular growth of wheat was simply out of the question, and barley grew to become the staple of the Sumerian diet for all classes and members of society.

Not only was barley essential for food, but it was also essential for the brewing of beer, a drink that held enormous importance during this period as it was drunk even more regularly than water. The people of Mesopotamia were remarkable engineers and had complex sewer piping systems under their streets several thousand years before many other parts of the world. From each household, waste traveled through underground pipes far away from the city—and then dumped into the river. This would undoubtedly have created a health disaster, with no source of reliable, healthy drinking water. Faced with a choice between dehydration or outbreaks of disease, the people of Sumer came up with an alternative option—drink beer. This meant that barley was the single most important source of sustenance, the center around which the entirety of Sumerian culture and civilization revolved.

As people developed a sense not only of individuality but of personal property, barley became an important source of wealth. Farming was a careful, precise undertaking, and if you had a good crop yield one year, you had the potential to become significant within society. Those who produced the most and the best quality barley would eventually accumulate the most wealth and importance. As wealth accumulated, people could afford to acquire larger plots of land for farming, producing even more barley, their social standing skyrocketing as a result. People would come to rely upon these individuals, and they would find themselves in the position to make important decisions. Over time, they would even hold enough wealth to pay others to work their fields for them, freeing up time to focus on their personal pursuits—the cultivation of the individual, and the individual's importance within the running of a city.

It was not merely barley that led to this change, of course. The fall of the "old ways" will have led to vacant spaces in society, and conflict between individuals to fill those spaces. The people of Sumer would have developed hierarchies based upon weakness and strength, and the ability to contribute to the running of society. These factors, among no doubt numerous others, coalesced to create tightly bound city-states governed largely by a wealthy class, the very early step toward the introduction of kingship in society. The sale of land increased, the trade of commodities and luxury goods grew dramatically, as wealthy individuals found themselves with time and resources to spare. Even though the temples maintained significant power in society over this period, the rise of a wealthy class created a new, more practical political body, rivaling and eventually surpassing the temples in importance.

The Lugal of Kish

The wealthiest of cities, which were typically those with the most fertile farmland, would also be the most common target for raiders from the steppe—the long belt of grassland extending from Hungary to Manchuria, over 5,000 miles. The steppe was a fantastic place for hunting and grazing livestock such as sheep and cattle, thus providing the cities on its border with a regular supply of meat. Raiders would come down from the hills to loot and pillage in the fertile, rich lands near the steppe, and it was the powerful city of Kish that was most often targeted.

The targeting of Kish was in part due to its location near where the two rivers were at their closest, and as such, the city controlled large amounts of fertile farmland. It was a rich city, and it was the problem posed by the raiders that would form one of the significant catalysts in the establishment of kingship. Rising to the top in Sumerian society did not come without obligations—as the old saying goes, with great power comes great responsibility. It was ultimately the leaders who were looked to for protection and guidance in times of conflict, and it was these leaders who, in time, would provide organized resistance against the barbarian raiders.

While small attacks could have been staved off by farmers and common folk wielding basic stone tools, larger parties were not so easily defeated and required the defense of organized, trained men with effective arms. The working class could never hope to organize such a defensive force, nor would they have the time to train while also maintaining the fields and looking after their families—a dedicated defensive force was necessary. It was the *Lugalene*, or the "big men" of the city, who would have the funds and the time to organize a defense. Some of the *Lugalene* would have even provided men from their households to act as standing soldiers for the city; over time these defensive groups evolved into genuine armies.

Eventually, one *Lugal* among the many would rise to the top and take his place as the effective 'warlord' of the city. Due to the pressure from the regular raids, it was Kish that became one of the earliest seats for a *Lugal*, rising to dominance through a standing army and immense wealth. Over time, the *Lugal* of a city would have turned away from merely defending and instead put his army to use acquiring territory and establishing dominance over other nearby cities and settlements. Kish in particular was known for its tendency to prevent its neighbors from growing too powerful. In fact, with Kish being the original seat of kingship and the dominant city of its time, the phrase "*Lugal* of Kish" became the accepted title used by those who wished to claim some form of hegemony over the region of Sumer. That said, other cities followed the example of Kish and quickly gained their own *Lugal* and armies. Before long, the city of Uruk gained enough manpower to rival and eventually overthrow Kish as the dominant city in Sumer.

From Lugal to Monarch

The passing of the kingship from Kish to Uruk signified an immense change in the political landscape of Sumer. The *Sumerian King List*, a document discovered in several editions across Mesopotamia and listing the rulers of Sumer from the establishment of Eridu to the kingship in Isin, lists a series of exchanges between cities as powerful *Lugal* challenge one another for regional dominance. Kingship had been bestowed from heaven upon Kish, but, not unlike the Chinese concept of the Mandate of Heaven, it appears the kingship could be rescinded and passed on to somebody else. Kingship descended from heaven to Kish, and then after a lengthy list of absurdly long-lived monarchs, Kish was defeated, and the kingship moved to Eanna (Uruk). From Uruk, the kingship was taken to

Ur; from Ur, it went to Awan; from Awan, back to Kish.

So it went, according to the king list, for an absurdly long time—while some rulers of ancient Sumer ruled only for a short period, others ruled far, far longer. Etana of Kish, for example, "ascended to heaven and put all countries in order, became king; he ruled for 1,500 years" (Livius.org, 2020). The kingship in Kish is professed to have lasted 23,310 years, 3 months and 3 1/2 days, spread between 23 kings. This means that, on average, each king of Kish ruled for around 1,000 years.

The king list outlines the origins of Sumerian dynasties, although it is important to note that the rulers rarely shared common blood, and each dynasty was defined more by the city than by the family lineage. The idea of hereditary monarchs, or even designated heirs, came about much later. The struggle for power between cities and between the men who ran them was bitter and constant—political careers were short-lived, as were, at times, the politicians themselves.

One unique perspective held by the Sumerians, however, is that both politics and war were not human pursuits; they were instead under the jurisdiction of the gods. Each city had its own god: Eridu had Enki, Uruk had Inanna, Nippur had Enlil. Wars may have been fought between armies of men, but the disputes were between the gods, merely using men as a tool in their conflicts. As a result, when two cities fought, such as Lagash and Umar, who engaged in repeated warfare over disputed land, the disagreement was, in fact, one between Ningirsu of Lagash and Shara of Umar, each of whom felt it was their right to the land in question—and to dominion over Sumer as a whole.

The one big difference between warlords and monarchs, irrespective of the power they may wield or how they may wield it, is the way they are viewed by others. A warlord may be powerful, with large armies at his disposal, able to issue decrees when and where he should choose, but he is still very much a human figure. Warlords maintain positions of power simply because of their control—their resources, their armies, the fear they instill in those they rule over. A monarch, at least traditionally, based their rule on something more altogether otherworldly—a divine bestowal of power, a religious confirmation of their right to rule. The emperors of China ruled under the Mandate of Heaven, legitimacy affirmed by a spiritual or religious force; in Europe, the "divine right of kings" dictates the monarchic authority derives from God and cannot be questioned. People need a reason to believe that the ruler, whoever they may be, is legitimately better than everybody else and genuinely deserves the power they hold. As such, the monarch must give the people a sign that their authority is divine.

In Sumer, it was no different, although the actual details of this move from *Lugal* to divine ruler are uncertain. What we do know is that in the city of Ur, for a short period, human sacrifices were made in the tombs of the deceased rulers, with skeletons found scattered across the floor, surrounded by a wealth of treasures rivaling even the tomb of Tutankhamen. Whether these sacrifices were willing or forced is up for debate, though Sir Leonard Woolley, who was involved in their discovery, believed them to be willing volunteers. He described a procession, likely made up of the court of the deceased ruler, entering a huge open pit with walls and doors covered in mats. Men, women, and soldiers would have been included, from slaves to decorated military commanders. Brightly colored garments, often ordained with lapis lazuli, were worn—only the best for the city's ruler. Even musicians would have accompanied the procession, carrying their instruments. Soldiers would follow up at the rear, guarding the entrance. Each of the volunteers would have brought with them a small clay cup. It was probable there were words spoken, likely entreaties to the gods, and the musicians would have played, before each of the volunteers filled their cup with poison and consumed it willingly and joyfully, following their great ruler into the underworld.

It is important to note that Woolley was being somewhat creative with his account, visualizing possibility as opposed to describing something for which there was solid evidence. Even so, whether willing or not, human sacrifices in the tombs of rulers symbolize a significant transition from the rule of mortal, human figures to the rule of something divine. Convincing the populace to accept the killing of their friends, family members, or even simply other city dwellers is no easy feat, and is most often seen in religious ceremonies intended to appease deities.

To have them sacrificed and left in the tomb of a mortal human demonstrates a drastic change in the way the people of Ur thought about their rulers. The graves were representative of attempts by the leadership of Ur to demonstrate their divine status, to combine state power with some form of supernatural authority. In doing so, they were able to assert the legitimacy of their rule. As Ur was the dominant city of Sumer at the time, it set an example for others to follow—the practice must have had a profound enough effect to make a continuation of the practice elsewhere unwarranted. It is believed that this was the moment when the rulers of Ur, and in turn, the rulers of Sumer, moved from simply *Lugal* to monarchs—the moment when kingship truly descended from heaven.

Chapter 2: The First Empire (ca. 2350-2150 BCE)

Prelude: The Conquests of Lugalzagesi

Sometime around 2400 BCE, a new sort of ruler rose to prominence in the city of Lagash. Urukagina, usurping the throne during a time of internal dissatisfaction, had a new approach to ruling his subjects—one that was less about fear or worship, and more about love. Urukagina appeared to have one thing in mind—to reform the city of Lagash so dramatically that his people would love him with all their hearts. Whether his motive was one of securing power, or that he genuinely wanted to ensure his people were living happy, comfortable lives, it is hard to say. What is abundantly clear, however, is that upon his ascension, the bureaucracy in Lagash was corrupt and crumbling. Taxes were high. The previous ruler had confiscated large amounts of land for himself and his family. There were additional charges to almost everything, from divorces to the shearing of sheep, and those additional charges were pocketed by the ruler and his ministers. Even burial rites came at an absurd cost, over 400 loaves of bread and 7 jars of beer paid to the priest and his assistant. Needless to say, the people were not happy.

Urukagina's legitimacy as a ruler was based on the rescue of his people from the domination of both the temple and his predecessor. He uncovered and put a stop to corruption throughout the bureaucracy, dedicating his time not to conquests and regional domination, but the well-being of his subjects. It seems probable that Urukagina was a good man, well-loved and respected, and would have had a long and successful reign ahead of him, were it not for the ambitions of another new ruler in the neighboring city of Umma.

Lugalzagesi of Umma was an ambitious man. Umma and Lagash had long been rivals, engaging in warfare originally over disputed territory, and had traded blows often over the past century. It was during a lull in conflict, however, while Urukagina was reforming his city, that Lugalzagesi saw an opportunity to build up his forces and strike a decisive blow. Lagash had often bested Umma, and it was perhaps this bitterness that drove forward the city's new ruler. The story of Urukagina goes to show that simply being a good ruler does not protect you from conquest and destruction. Urukagina's reign over Lagash lasted only a short eight years.

The fall of Lagash was condemned by many. Urukagina had been considered a good man, and Lugalzagesi was cursed by many for his crushing blow over his rival. Kriwaczek (2010) records a lament from the time:

The ruler of Umma has set fire to the temple of Antasurra; he has carried away the silver and the lapis lazuli... He has shed blood in the temple of the goddess Nanshe; he has carried away the precious metal and the precious stones... The Man of Umma, by despoiling Lagash, has committed a sin against the god Ningirsu... May the hand that he dared to raise against Ningirsu be cut off. There was no fault in Urukagina, King of Lagash. May Nisaba, the goddess of Lugalzagesi, ruler of Umma, make him bear his mortal sin upon his neck. (p. 100)

Lagash was merely the beginning. Lugalzagesi went on to conquer not only his neighbor but also the cities of Kish, Ur, Nippur, Larsa, and Uruk. He took the latter as his capital and declared hegemony over the states of Sumer. While his claims of controlling the entirety of the Fertile Crescent appear greatly exaggerated, there is little doubt that Lugalzagesi was the catalyst for something great. Little did he know that, upon deposing the ruler of Kish, he laid the foundations for the first empire in human history.

Sargon of Akkad

By this point in Mesopotamian history, there had been temple rulers, *Lugalene*, monarchs ruling from strength and fear, and even a monarch who sought the approval and love of his people. The trouble with all of these systems of leadership is that they could only succeed over a limited scope. Both love and fear go a long way, but perhaps not so far as to bind together a vast empire. As such, the regional rule of most previous kings had been limited to a selection of cities over a small area. Following the fall of Kish to Lugalzagesi, however, a new leader rose to prominence, and with him came a new form of leadership—one based on hero-worship rather than fear or love. This man was Sargon, and he founded the first empire in human history.

When one thinks of an empire, several things come to mind. Firstly, we think of emperors, usually monarchical rulers who appear in higher stead than a simple king or queen. Secondly, we think of vast swathes of land under the rule of a single governing body. The one thread that runs through all historical empires is that it contains not merely one culture or people, but many different groups, all brought together under a single administration. The Roman Empire ruled over many different cultures across Europe, Africa, and Asia; the Mongol Empire ruled an even greater number, stretching from the Far East to Asia Minor and ruling over China, Persia, and the steppe cultures. The British Empire ruled over even more cultures and peoples, stretching around the entire globe. To be the ruler of an empire is to rule over people who are not your own, alongside those who are.

Sargon was believed to be the cup-bearer to the Ur-Zababa, who ruled over Kish before the conquests of Lugalzagesi. Due to his quick rise following the deposition of his king, chances are that Sargon had long nurtured a desire for power. The role of cup-bearer was one of great importance and would have provided Sargon with the connections and funds needed to entice a considerable number of loyal followers. Whether he seized power and marched south under the guise of revenge, or if he was simply opportunistic, is difficult to say. Regardless of his apparent motivations, however, Sargon knew what he was doing, and before long he had captured Uruk and Lugalzagesi.

It was the conquest of Uruk that brought Sargon into power. However, despite vanquishing his opponent, he also had to contend with many Sumerian cities attempting to establish their freedom following the original conqueror's death. Freed from the yoke of Lugalzagesi, they hoped to maintain independence and saw the opportunity to do so. Sargon proved an efficient conqueror, however, and before long he had Sumer in the palm of his hand. In fact, not satisfied with ruling only Sumer, Sargon set about conquering neighboring territories, bringing the southern Sumerians and the northern Semites together under a single administration. He set out to build a vast empire, spreading far beyond the two rivers. It is said that he was victorious in 34 battles, even seizing the lands of the Elamites on the far bank of the Tigris, the city of Mari in north, and even pushing into the lands of the Amorites, whose connection to Mesopotamia would become significant hundreds of years later, as would the small city of Ashur, conquered on the northern banks of the Tigris. It is even suggested that Sargon of Akkad may have ventured into Asia Minor, although any success in the region would have been limited.

Sargon himself was, in fact, a Semite as opposed to a Sumerian, but as emperor over both peoples, he walked a lonely path between cultures. It was perhaps as a Semite living among Sumerians that Sargon had developed the mindset required to rule over many, the ability to understand people of various backgrounds and cultures. Whatever the case may be, Sargon knew that to establish himself as a new kind of ruler, to separate himself from both Ur-Zababa and Lugalzagesi, and to appeal not merely to the subculture of Kish but people the world over, he was required to create a new center of power.

Akkad (the Semitic name for the city; it was called Agade in Sumerian), founded by Sargon upon the establishment of his new empire, was to become the center of the Mesopotamian world. It was from Akkad not only that the name of the empire was derived (Akkadian Empire) but also that of the language spoken by many of its people, a language that was still spoken by inhabitants of the area many years later under the Assyrian and Babylonian empires.

For widespread appeal, Sargon was required to rethink kingship. The people of a nation or a city are typically bound to their ruler by a shared culture, language, or priority. To rule over many, a ruler had to establish themselves as universally acceptable, transcending typical ideas of belonging and culture. It could be a very lonely undertaking, requiring a lot of psychological fortitude, to no longer see yourself as part of a pre-established group. To make others see you that way as well requires a new kind of legitimacy, one that appeals to all.

The foundation of Akkad was the beginning of this separation, but it was to continue. Sargon had to cultivate an image of himself as a heroic figure, worthy of adulation and worship. While remaining a man, Sargon had to step into the role of a god, founding a city himself as opposed to inheriting one from a deity. Even his name was fabricated, meaning "true king"; his true name remains unknown. He created a backstory that accentuated his humble origins and avoided any particular political affiliations. In a story reminiscent of that of Moses, yet occurring much earlier, Sargon was said to have been conceived in secret by a priestess and then set upon a river in a basket of rushes, bore downstream until discovered by Akki, who raised him.

Regarded by later generations as semi-divine, Sargon's name was even called upon by later rulers to provide a sense of legitimacy to their rule. In fact, Sargon still offers a sense of legitimacy to this very day. In 1990, during the International Babylon Festival, Iraqi President Saddam Hussein celebrated his 53rd birthday in his home village with lavish festivities owing more than a little to the origin story of the great Akkadian emperor. A wooden cabin was wheeled into the street, before which numerous people dressed in ancient Mesopotamian costumes prostrated themselves as the door opened to reveal a baby in a basket, floating down a stream. The baby was representative of Hussein, but it called on the legitimacy offered by a connection to Sargon of Akkad. The longevity of Sargon's importance serves to demonstrate just how significant he was in the history not only of Mesopotamia but of the world as a whole, providing a model for future nations and empires thousands of years later.

The Rise and Fall of Gods

To describe the Bronze Age Akkadian empire as supplanting the role of religion and the gods in Mesopotamian society may be going a stretch too far, but Sargon's conquests had significant, long-term effects on the practice of religion and worship across his empire and into the future. He did not try to frame himself as an actual deity, rather a semi-divine hero not unlike those we have seen in the Greek Bronze Age—Heracles, Perseus, Achilles—those who had created a cult-like following of worshippers in recognition of their inhuman achievements.

In fact, the Akkadian period holds many parallels to the Greek age of heroes, where the gods, who had been directly involved in the lives of humans, took a step backward, retreating to Mount Olympus, and yet remaining connected to the world usually through Demi-gods and heroes such as those mentioned previously. Sargon's role as city-founder, and the man who tied a multicultural empire together, usurped the role of the city-founding god or the collective deity. This is not to imply that the gods were no longer important in Mesopotamian society; more they were now less connected, ruling from afar—that the new Akkadian empire was an empire not of gods but men.

This new relationship between people and gods can be seen in the artwork produced during this time. In the Stele of the Vultures, an earlier piece of artwork produced before the rise of Sargon to recognize one of Lagash's victories over Umma (before the rise of Lugalzagesi), the gods play a central role: a row of soldiers, led by a *Lugal*, are dwarfed by the enormous figure of the god Ningirsu who holds the captured enemy forces in his net. By contrast, a later stele depicts Sargon's third successor and grandson, Naram-Sin, in his victory over the Lullubi people of Zagros. In this piece, it is Naram-Sin who takes center stage, even wearing the horned helmet representative of divinity. The gods, while still present, are represented by mere stars in the sky.

Another interesting feature of Naram-Sin's stele is the composition of the image. The Stele of the Vultures is organized not unlike a comic strip, a series of events to be read as though part of a story, moving across the page, divided to represent new lines of 'text.' Naram-Sin's stele is entirely different, reminiscent more of a photograph than a story, a snapshot in time, a unified composition—a picture. This dramatic change in depictions not only suggests actual writing may have supplanted artworks and steles as a means of recording a series of events, but provides a general example of just how much the culture had changed in the first hundred or so years of the Akkadian empire.

In the new world of Sargon and Naram-Sin, humanity was no longer the tools of the divine. No more were the feuds and disagreements of the gods seen as part of the 'real' world, humanity's squabbles a mere shadow. Humans filled the shoes of the gods, ruling their cities and making decisions, not for some deity, but themselves. The focus of life had firmly shifted to the human world, and it would remain that way far into the future.

Naram-Sin is often considered equal, if not greater, in importance to Sargon in the history of Mesopotamia. He was also the final great Akkadian ruler, in power from 2261 to 2224 BCE, and is the main character in numerous stories over the following millennia—one in particular, *The Curse of Agade*, depicting him not as a great ruler but as the destroyer of Akkad, inviting divine punishment through impious acts. While this is merely fiction, Naram-Sin was likely chosen as the main character of this legend in part due to this immense fame, and in part due to the empire's gradual collapse in the wake of his death.

It was during the rule of Naram-Sin that the Akkadian Empire reached its zenith, and the powerful ruler certainly acted the part. He is depicted as a proud, confident, and arrogant ruler, proclaiming himself the "King of all four corners of the universe" — a line borrowed from his grandfather, Sargon. That said, Naram-Sin went one step further and deified himself, even going so far as to sign documents with a god's seal. According to Kramer (1971):

Naram-Sin... raised Agade to new heights of power and glory... His military successes were numerous and prodigious: he defeated a powerful coalition of rebellious kings from Sumer and the surrounding lands; he conquered the region to the west as far as the Mediterranean Sea and Taurus and Amanus ranges; he extended his dominion into Armenia and erected his statue of victory near modern Dierbakir; he fought the Lullubi in the northern Zagros ranges and commemorated his victory with a magnificent stele; he turned Elam into a partially Semitized vassal-state and constructed numerous buildings in Susa; he brought booty from Magan after defeating its king Manium, whom some scholars have identified with the renowned Menes of Egypt. (p. 62)

Despite his successes, however, Naram-Sin would forever remain associated with the fall of the empire. Following his death in 2224 BCE, he was succeeded by his son, Shar-Kali-Sharri, who ruled for 25 years. As with his predecessors, Shar-Kali-Sharri began his reign by stamping out numerous revolts across the empire; however, unlike those who came before, he failed to maintain peace and order, and the empire's borders were constantly under attack.

Whether the collapse was due to Shar-Kali-Sharri's incompetence, or to the unfortunate state of the empire he had inherited, is up for debate. However, it does appear that bad luck played a significant role, with invasions, border-wars, climate change, and famine eventually inspiring *The Curse of Agade*, with Shar-Kali-Sharri most likely serving as the true inspiration.

His death in 2198 BCE spelled the end of the Sargonic dynasty and was followed by several years of conflict as four rivals fought for control over the empire. When the dust settled, a new king, Dudu, held power in Akkad, but the empire was greatly diminished. Dudu and his successor ruled between 2189–2154 BCE, but the glorious days of the Akkadian empire were well and truly over. Following the collapse, Mesopotamia found itself thrust into a dark age. The self-styled gods had fallen, their creation in ruins. This period of conflict and disunity lasted until 2112 BCE when a new dynasty rose from the ashes—the kingship had returned to Ur.

Chapter 3: Sumer Restored (ca. 2119-2004 BCE)

More often than not, it is the most progressive societies that prove the most vulnerable. Progressive structures are essential for moving forward, for innovation, for creation, and for reform, but as they delve into unknown territory they encounter new problems for which there are no predefined solutions. Such was the case for the first empire in history. A combination of climate change and conflict put such pressure on the Akkadian borders that it simply collapsed in on itself. It was not designed with such struggles in mind.

During the dark age that followed, the most well-known ruler, Gudea of Lagash, did not take on the title of *Lugal* but instead referred to himself simply as an *Ensi*—a governor. He was a pious figure, building temples, bowing and scraping before the gods of old, demonstrating respect and recognition for the deities which came before Sargon and the Akkadians. While he was, by all accounts, a great man, Gudea of Lagash was also an ideal illustration of the attitudes of his time—and of all times following such a cataclysmic fall. Gudea represented the conservative attitude, a return to the old ways, the retreat into the safe burrow of traditional practices. He was no Sargon, no Naram-Sin. He returned to the old religion and restored the responsibility of war and politics to their rightful place: the gods.

It seems like a natural response to such trying times. Turning to gods, repenting the sins of the impious rulers, seeking a divine explanation for why such tragedy has befallen so many people. One need only look to *The Curse of Agade* to see this attitude made manifest. After all, if the gods bestow all rewards, if they sit in the heavens and make decisions about the world of men, they must also be responsible, and have reasons for, the tragedies and disasters that occur.

During this period, it was the Guti who ruled— barbarians from the Zagros Mountains who had seized upon the opportunity granted by a weak state and invaded from the east. The *Sumerian King List* suggests the Guti held power in Mesopotamia for several generations after the fall of Akkad. They were likely driven down from their mountains by the same famines and climate changes that contributed so significantly to the weakening of Akkadian control on the region.

The Guti had failed to restore the old practices of statecraft and administration which had worked so well for the Akkadians, instead allowing the many facets of imperial bureaucracy to fall into disrepair. Weeds and grass grew over roads, towns, and cities were neglected. They certainly did not hold the same understanding of engineering and public sewer systems as the previous rulers had, and made no efforts to appease the local populations through religion. It was apparent that it would only be a matter of time before the civilized cities of the south amassed their strength and struck once again into the heart of Mesopotamia, clearing the land of the invaders.

It was Utu-Hegal of Uruk who claimed to rid Mesopotamia of the Guti once and for all. He most likely prepared his revolt against the new overlords for many months, perhaps even years, gathering supporters and enlisting the help not only of his people but of the divine. In fact, Utu-Hegal made sure to offer Enlil, the supreme god, much of the credit for the vanquishing of the Guti (although of course not *all* of it), and claimed Inanna as a patron-goddess. This was, after all, not the time for progressive gestures. Utu-Hegal, as the leader of Uruk, had a responsibility to appease the gods and the god-fearing among his people.

Upon gathering his forces, Utu-Hegal marched north. He paused on his way to receive envoys from the Guti, and subsequently placed them in chains, before routing the enemy and destroying their forces. The Guti king fled with his family to a nearby town, but he was captured and handed over by citizens who sensed a change in the god's favor. Utu-Hegal "put handcuffs and a blindfold on him. Before Utu (the sun god), Utu-Hegal made him lie at his feet and placed his foot on his neck... He brought back the kingship to Sumer" (Kriwaczek, 2010, p. 130).

The accuracy of this story remains uncertain. States, especially new or returned states, make efforts to legitimize their ruler through origin stories and propaganda. In fact, it is believed that the *Sumerian King List*, first compiled around this time, was created to assert the legitimacy of Utu-Hegal's rule, demonstrating his connection to a long line of Sumerian rulers back to and even preceding the Flood.

However, there is an alternative explanation for this story. Following the resurgence of Sumer, there appears to have been a hasty recording of stories, records, myths, and legends, leading some to suggest that the shock of the fall of Akkad and the conquests of the Guti made Sumerians realize the fragility of their traditions and history, until that point having been largely recited orally. This is suggested by the inclusion of, and focus on, many mythical heroes (such as Gilgamesh) and deities in the recorded documents from this time, as opposed to strictly factual, human accounts. This is reminiscent of the Quran, which was first written after many of those who had it memorized were killed. This would suggest not political persuasion, but preservation, may have been the guiding factor in the recording of not only Utu-Hegal's defeat of the Guti, but of many other texts first written around this time. Regardless of the motivations, we know one thing for certain—around the year 2100 BCE, Sumer began the process of putting itself back together.

Despite Utu-Hegal's efforts to rid Mesopotamia of the Guti, he was unsuccessful in establishing a dynasty or a lasting power base in his city of Uruk. When Utu-Hegal died (following a reign of between 7-427 years, depending upon what source you consult), powerful men took advantage of the power vacuum and seized control of the region. The kingship was taken to Ur.

The Third Dynasty of Ur

The third dynasty of Ur, or Ur III as it is often known, became the foundation for the emerging Sumerian empire, which ruled the region between 2112 and 2004 BCE. The empire, often referred to as the Neo-Sumerian Empire, not only signified the restoration of power to the old base of Sumer, nor even a golden age for the great city of Ur. The Neo-Sumerian Empire was one of the most unusual and surprising forms of administration in the ancient world, a great experiment of sorts that had more in common with the Soviet Union than it did with the Akkadians preceding it.

Founded by Ur-Nammu, the nephew of Utu-Hegal, Ur III controlled much of the Mesopotamian plain, with formally independent cities becoming provinces or vassal territories, paying taxes to the central administration. The Sumerian language once again became the language of administration, although Akkadian remained spoken on the streets of many cities.

Scholarship on the Neo-Sumerian period has often believed the administration was entirely obsessed with bureaucracy, but this is largely to do with the locations of the archaeological excavations. Most of the digs have been pursuing rare and valuable items, and as such temples and palaces have been prioritized over other parts of cities. As such, it has had an impact on the portrayal of the empire, with ordinary, everyday life remaining unreflected. That said, the Neo-Sumerian Empire did indeed have an unusual, perhaps even radical, perspective on bureaucracy, which is even more surprising when you consider their place in history, long before even the early biblical tales of the origins of western society in Greece or Rome.

The structure of society in the Neo-Sumerian Empire was remarkably similar to that of Soviet or Maoist communism. It differed in many respects, especially regarding religious belief, but it was defined by the totalitarian ideologies used to justify economic and social arrangements. Put simply, the state took from each according to ability, and gave to each in accordance with need—although as usual, need and ability had to be decided by somebody, and more often than not one party or another would find themselves benefiting above others.

The individual had no voice, and society was structured not around citizens but groups or small communities, largely defined by ethnicity, family, or belief. The state owned all land and the means of production, and each individual was obliged to serve the state for at least part of the year. Society revolved around the concept of *Bala*, whereby each province or city would pay a certain amount in grain or livestock to a central resource pool, from which each could then draw from as needed. The amount contributed could vary, but could at times exceed 50% of a province's production for a year.

In fact, the Neo-Sumerians went even further than the communists may have by keeping detailed records of each and every individual's contributions and rewards. Those of the lower classes, such as the slaves and workers of little skill, were considered to be state property. They had no purpose aside from providing labor to the city each and every day. Supervisors, on the other hand, had it very differently. Their performance was measured with extreme detail, and then scrutinized intensely. Their goods, materials, and labors, including metals, wool, and grains (all provided by the state), were measured and converted into equivalent "worker days." This was contrasted with the credit— namely, the production output, be that quality of flour, number of textiles woven; as it was different depending upon the team. Again, an equivalent in worker-days was calculated, even making room for time spent on side-projects such as repairs or urgent, external jobs, as well as the workers' yearly leave, averaging around 35 days a year for men and 55 for women.

The expected production was much higher than was possible, and surpluses were extremely rare. Many supervisors would end up with considerable debts to the state, which could have been called in at any point. If a supervisor was to die before paying up, his debts would fall to his descendants, who may have been required to sell themselves into slavery to raise the funds.

Another element of Neo-Sumerian administration that is particularly interesting is their use of invalids and the disabled. Everybody had their place in society, filling some role or another. This may have simply been an attempt to exploit every last possible means of production, but may also have been intended to offer a place in society to those who could not hope to otherwise compete or succeed.

The new style of government worked well for a time. Uniformity was established across the empire—a national curriculum was designed for scribal training, weights and measures were standardized and remained so for the rest of Mesopotamian history. Even an imperial calendar was created, used for all administrative documents aside from purely local matters. Even an early code of laws was created, listing various crimes and disagreements and the resolutions or punishments for each. Capital crimes were listed as murder, robbery, the deflowering of another man's wife, or adultery (when committed by a woman), whereas other crimes had a prescribed quantity of silver to be paid, differing depending upon severity. While this legal system was not as complete as that of Hammurabi in the second millennium BCE, it went a long way toward standardizing punishments and bringing all cities and regions under a single law code.

Ideology and Personality

This ability to bring everybody together under one uniform banner was quite remarkable. The government in Ur managed to override local traditions across the empire and had a tight grip on institutions and practices throughout cities under its jurisdiction. They were obsessed with the regulation of everything in society. Society was structured to have a single, father-like figure on the throne, with everybody else spread out below him in the shape of a pyramid, a hierarchy based on and held together by the complex web of ability, contribution, and reward. Such a complex and inorganic state, however, needs something to hold it together, something beyond mere ideology. It is a common fact of life that humans tend toward the conservative, looking back on the societies of their youth as ideal and struggling to assimilate into new societies later in life. To overcome this tendency, the Sumerian king needed to create something that would bind his people together, something that would overpower this tendency toward social inertia.

The solution was to generate adulation and awe from the people of the empire. The truth is, states based on power can last for centuries without too much struggle, so long as they allow people to retain their culture and traditions. Ideological states, especially those that aim to control the economic structure of society, struggle to last even half that long. They become so obsessed with the control of the mindset of their population that they are unable to focus on defending themselves from outsiders, and the grip often falters first from the inside. To tie people together, a ruler needs to create a reminder of their power, legitimacy, and ideology.

Ur-Nammu, the first king of the Neo-Sumerians, came up with a plan to remind the people of his greatness on a daily basis. It is, in fact, one of the first things that springs to mind when one thinks of Sumer and Mesopotamia—the Ziggurat of Ur.

Ziggurats were magnificent structures, smaller than the Pyramids of Giza and yet no less impressive, rising high above the surrounding city and built in three immense levels. The lowest level was the widest, and a second, slightly smaller level was built above, leaving room for a walkway around the outside and terraces at each side. The third level was a temple, closest to the sky. The Ziggurat of Ur, and other ziggurats which came to rise from other cities across Sumer, were designed to momentarily bring the human and the divine world together. While the Ziggurat of Ur remained incomplete upon his death, Ur-Nammu had created a monumental reminder of his divinity, the sort of structure that would attract people from miles around and spark the imagination of men and women for many thousands of years into the future.

There was one other method of maintaining an ideological state that is not only noticeable in Neo-Sumerian records, but also the Soviet state of the 20th century. The cult of personality has been used, in varying ways, for centuries, but a comparison between the worship of rulers like Shulgi, the second king of Ur III, and the adulation afforded to Stalin or Lenin, demonstrates a similar tactic used for similar reasons millennia apart.

Shulgi, like Naram-Sin of the Akkadians, declared himself a god during his reign. The actual purpose of this remains unclear, but it has been suggested that the deification was designed to create a figurehead to bind the people of the empire together. An ideological state cannot be maintained if the people are expected to believe in the *concepts* as they are. A populace tends to follow, or worship, a personality over an idea. The cults of Lenin and Stalin held the Soviet Union together, and while neither declared themselves to be gods as did Shulgi and his successors, their mummified bodies were kept on display, attracting pilgrims to this day. This form of worship amounted to a Soviet state religion, despite their atheistic ideology.

In *Babylon*, Kriwaczek (2010) presents two passages, one written as a chant in honor of Stalin in the 1930s, another for Shulgi in the third millennium BCE. Upon first glance, it is difficult to tell which passage is in honor of whom:

Who is as mighty as you, and who rivals you?

Who is there who from birth was as richly endowed with understanding as you?

May your heroism shine forth, and may your might be respectfully praised! (p. 143)

And the second:

Thou who broughtest man to birth.

Thou who fructifiest the earth,

Thou who restorest the centuries,

Thou who makest bloom the spring,

Thou who makest vibrate the musical chords...

Thou, splendour of my spring, O thou,

Sun reflected by millions of hearts. (p. 144)

It may come as some surprise that it is the first, in its somewhat more humble phrasing, that was written in honor of Shulgi, king of Sumer. The latter, far more dramatic, was written for the "Great Stalin, O leader of the peoples" in 1935. Comparing these together, the Neo-Sumerian Empire, in all of its communist-like glory, appears more reasonable, humble, and human, despite existing many thousands of years ago. Either way, Shulgi, king of Sumer, was the Neo-Sumerian culture and ideology made human— the glue that bound the empire together.

The Fall

Nothing lasts forever, and most controlled, ideological states last for very little time at all. The collapse of the Neo-Sumerians was not only inevitable but happened remarkably quickly. What sparked the decline is not certain, but it appeared that upon the ascension of King Ibbi Sin, the provincial regions began to detach themselves from central control. Within the first two years of his reign, taxes had ceased from the most distant provinces, and outlying cities had stopped dating documents using the official imperial calendar. This was the case across the entire empire by his ninth year. The outlying provinces declared independence. Vultures circled. Enemies amassed on the borders.

Semitic peoples in the west, known as Amorites, began raiding the lands along the Euphrates. During times of stability, the western Semites would enter the empire peacefully and in small numbers, but during times of weakness, they came in numbers and were well-armed. They seized patches of territory in the empire's west, and their attacks drove the price of grain up enormously. When the king in Ur asked one of his generals to secure wheat and barley from the north, the general informed him that due to the danger posed by raiders, he was not going to return the grain to Ur.

The final blow came not from the west, but the east. Once under Sumerian control, the new leader of Elam had risen and marched into southern Mesopotamia. Ur fell quickly, and King Ibbi Sin was carted off to Elam and never seen again. The Elamites occupied Ur for seven years before being driven out, but by this time the damage was well and truly done. Sumer fractured into individual city-states, this time ruled largely by Amorite chieftains or Sumerian warlords.

Ur was forsaken, the kingship rescinded. Sumer would never again reign supreme.

Chapter 4: Old Babylon (ca. 2000-1600 BCE)

Babylon is one of the most famous cities of the ancient world. Where places like Akkad, Kish, and Lagash are known almost exclusively to academics, with a few other Mesopotamian cities mentioned in the Old Testament, Babylon has secured a long-term position in the human imagination. Even those who do not know when Babylon flourished, or even why it is significant, still most likely recognize the name.

Babylon may have received its name from *Bab-Ilu*, the Gate of God. It is a city of biblical infamy, known for the exile of the Jews, described as the "mother of harlots and abomination of the earth" (Carroll & Prickett, 2008, Revelation 17:5). It is remembered by the Greeks as a city like any other, by the Rastafarians as the ultimate symbol of the oppression of Black people, and by the British of the Victorian Era as one of the most magnificent cities of ancient history. It is remembered differently by different people, but there is no doubt that it *is* remembered.

The trouble with Babylon is that much of its history cannot be studied in archaeological sources. In the time since the Old Babylonian Empire, the water table has risen to the point of preventing excavation beyond the later period of its occupation. The Babylon of King Hammurabi is lost to us, possibly forever. Even so, we have enough information from surrounding cities, and later periods, to build a detailed picture of what life in Babylon may have been like.

Babylon was a city founded by the Amorites, those who had invaded the Neo-Sumerian Empire from the west at the end of the last reign of Ur. In this sense, they represent a continuation of an old pattern—the crumbling of the old Mesopotamian centers of power and the occupation by external forces. However, unlike the Guti of times past, the Amorites recognized the benefit in continuing the traditions and practices of the Sumerian culture preceding them. As such, they were well positioned to form a new, dominant power in the region.

This did not happen overnight. For several centuries following the fall of the Neo-Sumerian Empire, westerners poured into Mesopotamia. In Akkadian, they were called the *Amurru*, but they did not all come from the same location, being made up of at least two distinct Semitic peoples. In addition, there were also foreigners entering the region from the north and the east.

Power bases were established and collapsed, cities rose and fell, fighting for domination between the two great rivers. Chaos reigned. Some cities had three or four kings in a single year. Monarchs would emerge as if from the earth, only to return to it no less swiftly. One interesting story tells of King Irra-Imitti of Isin who, fearing bad omens, placed the gardener Enlil-Bani on the throne with the intention that the gardener should suffer whatever fate had in store. Enlil-Bani was to be removed from the throne and killed when the period of misfortune had passed; instead, King Irra-Imitti himself died and Enlil-Bani refused to relinquish power. He ruled for almost 25 years, making him one of the longest-reigning monarchs of this period.

We have unique insight into this period through documents uncovered in Mari, a city captured by Hammurabi of Babylon before he established his empire. Thousands of clay tablets were uncovered, offering a glimpse of the thought processes and personalities of leaders of the time. One such man was Zimri-Lim of Mari, whose writings show us a man with a witty personality, a tendency toward the use of proverbs and social references as opposed to outright, crude humor. He was also a man with a vain streak, harassing servants for specific garments and fabrics, angered when his desires were not entertained. He was curious, traveling at length to neighboring regions, and was active in diplomacy and government affairs. Most significantly, however, Zimri-Lim of Mari was a pious man, with love for the gods and for religious festivals, and a keen interest in any signals the gods may have sent down to his realm.

This is just a small taste of the wealth of information the preserved tablets had to offer. Written largely informally, we can learn not merely of these people's day-to-day lives but their thoughts, feelings, vices, and values.

It was following the collapse of Mira, however, and presumably the death of Zimri-Lim, that the next great state revealed itself. Hammurabi, best known for his code of laws, was the sixth king in the first dynasty of Babylon but was to become the first king to rule over a Babylonian Empire proper following his conquest of southern Mesopotamian. As such, it was the Old Babylonian Era, led into glory and posterity by King Hammurabi, that emerged from the ruins left by the third dynasty of Ur.

King Hammurabi's Code

The code of laws attributed to Hammurabi was found not in Babylon, but the city of Susa. Upon the document, the king is shown to be receiving the laws from the god Shamash, whom to the Sumerians had been the sun god Utu, brother of Inanna. It begins with a preamble explaining the purpose of the document and proclaiming Hammurabi's greatness, "who like a father gave his people their birth" (Richardson, 2000, p. 123).

It is not a code of laws in the modern sense, rather providing a list of model cases, likely either drawn from real life or fabricated examples of crimes, covering upward of 280 judgments. Even commodities, prices, wages, and family law (including marriage, divorce, and incest) are included in the code. Considering our perspective on the ancient past, we may find some laws in Hammurabi's code to seem quite progressive, especially regarding women, as recorded by Kriwaczek (2010):

If a man wish [*sic*] to separate from a woman who has borne him children... he shall give that wife her dowry, and a part of the income from field, garden, and property, so that she can rear her children... She may then marry the man of her heart.

If a woman quarrel [*sic*] with her husband, and says: "You are not congenial to me," the reasons for her prejudice must be presented. If she is guiltless... but he leaves and neglects her, then no guilt attaches to this woman, she shall take her dowry and go back to her father's house. (p. 169)

Hammurabi's laws differed from those of Ur-Nammu in that retribution is more obviously on display. Where Ur-Nammu's laws proclaimed fines of varying amounts for most crimes, Hammurabi has a more direct "eye for an eye" approach to punishment—quite literally: "If a man has destroyed the sight of another similar person, they shall destroy his sight. If he has broken another man's bone, they shall break one of his bones." (Richardson, 2000, p. 105).

Some of these punishments may come across as extreme, but at the same time, they were effective as universal punishments. Babylon was a multi-ethnic society, differing enormously from the Sumer and Akkad of old where most members of society belonged to a single cultural identity, or several similar subcultures. Value systems differed between cultural groups, and as such, the subtlety of traditional cultural punishments would not have been effective, and an easy-to-understand code of laws was required. Where some people may not understand the idea of paying a fine for causing physical harm, the philosophy of "an eye for an eye" is simple to grasp no matter where you are from.

A New Society

The old division of cities, with an individual god residing in each, was now long gone; the age of empires had begun. At this point in history, there were two major powers: Babylon ruled the south of Mesopotamia, while the city of Ashur dominated the north. In each, people from numerous backgrounds mixed, offering their culture to the enhancement of society. It is often easy to imagine multicultural societies as a modern phenomenon, but such a belief would be misplaced. The mixing of cultures has been practiced throughout history and often signals a period of prosperity, glory, and acceptance.

Babylon had taken a drastic new approach to society following the collapse of the Neo-Babylonian Empire. Gone was the Sumerian obsession with collectivism, the old semi-communist practices of Ur III nothing more than a memory. Individualization returned in the Babylonian Empire to the point that society itself seemed to be nothing more than a collection of individuals, each pursuing his or her own means. Compared to days past, people became detached from one another. Privatization became a central tenet to society. In fact, Babylon of old was not too different from a capitalist society today, with banks, trading companies, loans, shares, mortgages, and investments all becoming part of everyday life.

While this encouraged the vast economic expansion that characterizes the western world today, it also resulted in high levels of debt and a dramatic increase in the gap between the wealthy and the impoverished. It was not uncommon for people to sell themselves, their children, or their siblings into slavery simply to fund debt repayments. Aware of this, Hammurabi ensured his law code considered the issue, proclaiming that anyone sold into slavery over a debt would be set free after working for three years, debts forgiven.

The language of Sumerian ceased to be spoken on a day-to-day basis among the masses, and instead became what Latin is for us today—a language of religion and scholarship, written but rarely spoken. It remained in use for more than a thousand years after this point, disappearing only after the fall of Mesopotamian civilization around 700 BCE, but it never again served as the common tongue of an empire.

One other area of society that changed dramatically during the Old Babylonian Era was education and scholarship. Education was a secular affair, perhaps in part due to the multi-ethnic society, and it was also extremely accessible—assuming you could afford to send your children for education rather than having them help with day-to-day tasks. Most poor people remained uneducated, but among the merchant and wealthy classes, literacy, and numeracy levels grew dramatically. The Babylonians were a very concrete people, studying mathematics and even science in detail, but their achievements often instead heaped upon the Greeks of antiquity due to their more theoretical approach. Many of the practices we attribute to Ancient Greece were, in fact, inherited first from Babylon. The Babylonians insisted upon the importance of the concrete over the abstract; they valued practice over theory.

Omen tables, while easily dismissed at first glance, were, in fact, an early Babylonian attempt at understanding the world from a scientific perspective. They recorded important events and noted any unusual occurrences from beforehand, hoping to find connections between signs and outcomes. They saw the world as based on natural laws, logical, rational, and not dictated by the whims of a god or gods. Through studying omens, they were trying to understand cause and effect—if X happens, Y is going to follow. The diviners themselves, far from relying upon spiritual guidance, believed they were approaching the world from an empirical perspective. While we may now look at their practices and laugh, it remains clear that, from their perspective, they were uncovering worldly truths, not merely seeking guidance from spirits and deities.

In medicine, also, the Babylonians excelled. There were two types of physicians in the cities of old Babylonia—the *ashipu*, specializing in omens and exorcisms, and the *asu*, who made diagnoses and offered medications. Physicians were so important to the Babylonian society that Hammurabi's code went so far as to dictate the fees paid to physicians for their services—as well as the punishments for when they failed. As in mathematics, they focused on a practical medical approach, leaving little in the way of medical theory, and thus differ once again from the Greeks who followed. ___

That said, they appeared to have a very in-depth understanding of medicine and health, evolving their beliefs through several hundred years of careful observations and experiments. Their prescriptions for certain health issues, while perhaps lacking the scientific understanding we have today, were remarkably accurate and effective. For example, slices of liver would be prescribed as a cure for night-blindness (the inability to see at night, despite perfect sight during daytime). Today, we understand that this condition is caused by a lack of vitamin A—something the liver is rich in.

Some practices are even still in use today, such as the draining of lungs in pneumonia patients, following a remarkably similar procedure to modern times. They even had an understanding of the spread of diseases, as is demonstrated in another letter, noted by Avery (2016):

I have heard that the lady Nanname has been taken ill. She has many contacts with the people of the palace... Now then, give severe orders that no one should drink from the cup where she drinks, no one should sit on the seat where she sits, no one should sleep in the bed where she sleeps... This disease is contagious. (p. 7)

The Fall of Old Babylon

There is little in the way of recorded history during the time of Old Babylon, and even less so in the way of personal accounts. With such a focus on the practical, abstract ideas such as opinions and retellings were largely dismissed as unnecessary. That is not to imply that speculative thought was entirely lacking in the Babylonian mind, more that it is difficult for us to identify and interpret. The unfortunate consequence of this is that we know little about the fall of the Old Babylonian Empire, and what we can devise from the sources we have is lacking in substance.

What we do know is that following Hammurabi, there were five more kings in the first dynasty of Babylon, each of which reigned for upward of 20 years. However, as was the case following the reign of Shulgi of Ur, and even Naram-Sin of Akkad, controlled territory began progressively to shrink following Hammurabi's death, with cities and land being seized by outsiders. Once again, foreigners crossed the borders, and for some reason, people appeared to leave cities en masse. The de-urbanization was dramatic, with many significant Sumerian cities losing vast numbers of their populations. Even great cities like Ur lost the majority of their citizens.

The final blow to the Old Babylonian Empire came from the north—specifically Anatolia, which was ruled at the time by the Hittites. A Hittite force was sent south through Mesopotamia, reaching the city of Babylon and shaking it, bringing the dynasty to an end. The Hittites had no desire to rule from Babylon and so quickly left, leaving an enormous power gap that was soon filled by the Kassites. The Kassites were an eastern people, and held power in Babylon for over 400 years, during which little advancement occurred.

That said, Kassite Babylon by no means reached the previous lows seen during the Guti occupation following the fall of the Akkadians or even the years between the Neo-Sumerian and the conquests of Hammurabi. Kassite Babylon entered a sort of cultural stasis, retaining elements of the old culture but improving on them little. Meanwhile, it was the Assyrians, based in the northern city of Ashur, who would dominate Mesopotamia.

Chapter 5: Assyria (ca. 1800-700 BCE)

The great empire of Assyria is subject to some of the most negative perceptions in the history of the world. It has often been categorized alongside the Mongolian Empire or the Third Reich in terms of the violence it represents. The ancient city of sin may surely be Babylon, but it was Assyria that was considered the state of evil.

But is this perception a fair one? The Assyrians were surely no worse than the Romans, who were comfortable displaying rotting corpses for miles along the Appian Way in response to rebellion, or to any number of other nations and empires through history whose creatively gruesome methods of capital punishment shock us to this day. In fact, in a world where we can even entertain the idea of killing hundreds of thousands of civilians with atomic weapons, it seems somewhat hypocritical to crown Assyria as the empire of violence. The Assyrians contributed enormously to literature, science, theology, mathematics, and engineering, and are even believed to have been inspirations for the great Greek poets of antiquity such as Homer and Hesiod. Their empire provided the template upon which all future empires were built, and they even led the way toward a monotheistic society.

This is not to suggest they were a peaceful people. What started as a merchant state in the north of Mesopotamia was, over time, transformed into a highly militarized, aggressive society with a severe justice system and even more severe treatment of women. Nonetheless, we can follow the Assyrian story from its origins to its precipice, from mercantile to military, to understand the forces that led to their transformation from a small state to the largest empire the world had yet seen.

The Merchant State

In the early years of the Old Babylonian Empire, or perhaps even earlier, before the conquests of Hammurabi, people settled in the region near where today's Syria, Iraq, and Turkey meet. This was fertile land, with plentiful rain, far from the arid farmland of the south which required the building of dams and canals to water the fields. These people inherited their culture from Babylon to the south, but rather than building an impressive imperial base and conquering surrounding territory, they appeared to spend their time focusing on trade and sale, establishing a base in the city of Ashur along the banks of the Tigris.

Early Assyria was made up of mostly small farming communities, the only major city in the area being Ashur itself. Ashur was known simply as "The City" by many of its inhabitants, and thus conjures images of Constantinople during the medieval period in terms of significance and prestige. The fortifications were monumental, and yet Ashur was located in a particularly dangerous region, surrounded by three major empires—the Hittites and Mitanni to the north and northwest and Babylon to the south, with Egypt at this point working its way up the eastern coastline of the Mediterranean. While there was much exchange between the empires and Assyria in ideas and technology, their location prevented them from becoming powerful, constantly suppressed on all sides by great strength.

During this early Assyrian period, the Amorites ruled in Babylon but following their fall to the Hittites and the Kassites it was Assyria that held the mantle of Mesopotamian culture, and they were very aware of this. They retained innumerable practices, leaving the pantheon almost unchanged aside from the supplanting of Marduk, the city god of Babylon and successor of Enlil, with Ashur, for whom their capital city was named. Despite this cultural debt to the south, the relationship with Babylon was ofttimes strained, and sometimes outright violent. The two nations, Assyria small but rising, Babylon on the decline under its Kassite overlords, competed fiercely in trade and prestige, and the Assyrians even assaulted the city of Babylon on multiple occasions. Despite this, the Assyrians would often attempt to make reparations to Babylon, and it is believed that there may have been two major factions vying for power through much of Assyrian history—the nationalist, anti-Babylonian powers, and the traditionalists who remained aware of their debts to their southern neighbor.

It was business and mercantile practice that drove early Assyria forward, and during this time their culture was almost incomparable to what it would later become. Merchants would travel across Anatolia to the north and northwest, setting up trading settlements to work and trade with the local communities. The wealthy Assyrian families would send out representatives to these trading communities, receiving goods from home, which they would trade for silver. The silver would then be sent back to the city.

Some men would marry local women, even father children, although they were permitted to divorce these women when their time at the communities came to an end, so long as they paid a fair compensation to the families and any possible children.

While private businesses had taken over from the old Akkadian and Sumerian state-based trading practices, there were still regulations on what could and could not be traded. Merchants would find themselves in trouble if they were caught transporting illegal goods. That said, the profits could be enormous, perhaps as a result of the risk involved in transporting goods across dangerous lands.

While Babylonian textiles were greatly desired and fetched a handsome price, their import from the south was not always reliable, and thus the Assyrians made efforts to create their own. Maintaining a high standard was of exceptional importance, as demonstrated by this letter from a merchant to his wife back in Ashur (Hirth, 2010):

Concerning the fine cloth that you sent me: you must make more like that and send it to me via Ashur-Idi. Then I will send you a half pound of silver. Have one side of the cloth combed, but not shaved smooth: it should be close-textured...

The other side must just be lightly combed. If it still looks fuzzy, it will have to be close shaved, like kutanu-cloth. (p. 225)

Women played an important role in this mercantile state, in dramatic contrast to their treatment only a few hundred years later under a transformed Assyria. They would supervise the production, loading, and dispatch of goods, and were comfortable making their opinions and feelings clear when communicating with their merchant husbands via letter. In one uncovered tablet, a woman writes to her husband: "Why do you keep writing to me: 'The textiles that you send me are always of bad quality!' Who is this man who lives in your house and criticizes the textiles that are brought to him?" (Kriwaczek, 2010, p. 203). Despite their role in society, however, it appears women were often neglected by their traveling husbands, being left with little funds or food while they remained in Ashur, overseeing the production of their husbands' goods.

However, within a few generations, the Assyrian way of life changed dramatically. What had been up until then a relatively peaceful, moderately progressive merchant state, took a sudden U-turn toward nationalism, militarization, and expansionism. The trading life ceased, and

Assyria transformed into the greatest of the Mesopotamian empires.

From Mercantile to Military

At some point around the middle of the second millennium BCE, catastrophe befell Assyria. The city was attacked by outsiders, rulers lost their territories and their bloodlines were extinguished. The subsequent years were defined by a series of illegitimate rulers rising from nowhere, as recorded in an unearthed list of Assyrian rulers: "Ashur-Dugul, son of a nobody, who had no title to the throne; he ruled for six years... the following six sons of nobodies ruled for periods of less than a year." (Kriwaczek, 2010, p. 204).

Assyria was too small and insignificant to stand up to the outside powers, especially Mitanni to the north, which sacked Ashur at one point and left with gold and silver doors to mount at the king's palace. The ruler of Assyria was forced into submission, and a long economic depression resulted. Through this period, the Assyrians came to understand the need to hold on to provinces and trading centers throughout their territory, lest their people and city fall into poverty. They came to see the world as a dangerous place, not least because they were crushed between four dangerous adversaries. It was the resulting anxiety and paranoia that would act as the catalyst in their transformation from an insignificant region, overshadowed by giants, to a regional superpower.

One of the ways we can observe this change is through the cylindrical seals used by the rich and powerful to identify themselves. While public presentation had always been significant in ancient Mesopotamia, cylindrical seals tend to show a more personal, honest representation of what an individual thought of himself (it was almost always men who used them). Seals from the early Assyrian period show men bowing before the gods and making offerings; later, these seals change to far more aggressive, dominant symbols which show men as impressive rulers or fighting with savage beasts that "fill the Assyrian seals with a world of fantastic vigour which seems untrammelled with any purpose to tell a story but only to picture the clash of mythological terrors against daemoniac champions of human kind." (Gadd, 1977, p. 47)

Assyria's lucky break ultimately came when the Hittites sacked the Mitannian capital, killing their ruler. As the empire fell, the Hittites and Assyrians divided up the land between them.

This time, the Assyrians had no intention of losing their newly gained territory, their militarized psychology having developed through years of political and diplomatic paranoia. They had gained enough land to grant them a place on the international stage, and the Assyrian king, Ashur-Uballit, wrote to the Egyptian Pharaoh Akhenaten in the mid-1300's BCE, pronouncing his new power, as quoted by Spar (1988):

Say to the king of the land of Egypt: Thus Ashur-uballit, the king of the land of (the god) Ashur. For you, your household, for your land, may all be well. I have sent my messenger to you to visit you and to visit your land. Up to now, my predecessors have not written; today, I have written to you. I send you a splendid chariot, 2 horses, and 1 date-stone of genuine lapis lazuli as your greeting gift. (p. 149-150)

Ashur-Uballit was polite, but there was little sign of the reverence usually offered to the Pharaoh of Egypt by other contemporary rulers. Later in his reign, Ashur-Uballit wrote again to the Pharaoh, in this letter referring to the ruler as his 'brother' and thus suggesting equal standing between them. The paranoia that had grown within the Assyrian state had left them extremely sensitive to even the mildest perceived slight, and they demanded equal standing among empires. When an insult was perceived, the Assyrian king was quite comfortable responding in kind, even to the most powerful ruler in the known world. "Is it from a great king, a gift such as this? Gold is dust in your land—one simply gathers it up... If in good faith your intention is friendship then send me much gold" (Kriwaczek, 2010, p. 207).

This newfound confidence was sure to raise eyebrows across the Middle East. In Babylon, the Kassite ruler was upset by the Assyrian contact with the Egyptian Pharaoh and made no efforts to disguise his displeasure. He demanded the Pharaoh reject the Assyrian envoys, claiming they were his own citizens and that he had not authorized their expedition to Egypt. That said, the Kassites in Babylon were clearly aware of the threat posed by their northern neighbor, managing to convince Ashur-Uballit to send one of his daughters south to marry the crown prince.

Years later, it was their son, half-Babylonian, half-Assyrian, who took up the throne in Babylon. However, Kassite nobles were apparently unhappy with the arrangement and revolted. Following the new Babylonian king's assassination, the king of Assyria rode south and seized the city, eliminating opposition and installing a puppet ruler. For the first time in history, it was now Ashur, and not Babylon, that held true power over Mesopotamia.

A New Culture

The struggle for preeminence in Mesopotamia lasted for many hundreds of years. It became somewhat simpler when the Hittites fell in the 12th century, and it was in 1120 BCE that the Assyrians reached their first peak when King Tiglath-Pileser I crossed the Euphrates to capture Carchemish. This victory was short-lived, however. Immense numbers of Aramaic-speaking camel herders and traders had been moving west, and around this time the numbers spiked further still. These immigrants seized land for themselves, carving slices from the edge of the Assyrian territory until, over time, the Assyrian empire was pushed all the way back to its homeland around Ashur. They remained confined in this point for nearly a century, and it was during this low point that the most dramatic changes in Assyrian society occurred.

Legal tablets dating from around the rule of Tiglath-Pileser show just how far the Assyrians had come from their peaceful, mercantile origins. The penalties laid out in these tablets are strikingly brutal, even when compared to

Hammurabi's "eye-for-an-eye" policies from earlier in the millennium, and nowhere is this more apparent than in the treatment of women. Women were targeted harshly and punished severely, especially when compared with the punishments received by men. Gruesome death penalties, horrific mutilations, and savage beatings were common punishments for various crimes. The sudden rise of misogyny in Assyria is both fascinating and horrifying. According to one of the tablets, if a women made efforts to receive an abortion (specifically, if she induced a miscarriage), upon her conviction she would have been impaled upon stakes and left to rot in the Assyrian sun. If she had died in the process of the abortion, however, it was her body that would be impaled, and she would receive no burial. In the event that she had fought with a man and injured one of his testicles, her finger would be cut off; if she injured both of them, or if the second became infected as a result of the original injury, they would go a little further: her eyes would be gouged from her head. If she should commit adultery with another man, they would both simply be killed; however, if the husband chose instead to slice off his wife's nose, he could then choose to brutally mutilate the face of the guilty man, and make him into a eunuch.

―

Needless to say, the Assyrian treatment of women (and men, to a lesser degree) was extreme. It is difficult to say exactly how often punishments of this severity were actually practiced, but it is clear simply from the document's existence that the Assyrian attitude had changed dramatically. Brutality, and especially that toward women, appeared to be a central virtue in society—"An inscription of Tiglath-Pileser, comparing the king to a hunter, who 'set out before the sun rose and marched three days' distance before dawn,' proudly claims that he 'cut open the wombs of the pregnant, he blinded infants.'" (Kriwaczek, 2010, p. 210). If anything, these horrific accounts appear to be tools of propaganda and manipulation, used to strike fear into enemies and the populace alike, not unlike practices used by the Mongols during their conquests in the 13th and 14th centuries CE where the horrific treatment of one city would encourage others to surrender without any resistance.

The treatment of women went further, in fact, and laid the foundations for some common practices across the region to this very day. It is at this point in history where we first encounter the veil, or specifically the forced covering of women in public in a style similar to today's hijab. Assyrian women of any respectable standing (such as a wife, widow, or daughter) were required to veil themselves in order to go out in public. They were permitted to use a shawl, robe, or mantle, so long as their hair and head was covered for modesty. Should a man's concubine go out into the street while accompanied by his wife, she would also veil herself, as would a prostitute whom a man had chosen to marry. A standard prostitute, however, was not permitted to wear a veil.

One major difference between Islamic and Assyrian practices is the division between those who must be veiled and those who must not. In Islamic tradition, all women wore veils, with no distinction between members of society. In Assyria, the wearing of a veil was restricted to 'respectable' women; those who veiled illegally were punished no less severely than those who should veil but did not. A female slave who veiled herself would be prosecuted and have her ears cut off. A veiled prostitute would also be arrested, have her clothing confiscated, and be flogged 50 times. A man who saw an illegally veiled woman was obliged to bring her in for prosecution, lest he also wished to be flogged, and more besides: "they shall pierce his ears, thread them with a cord, and tie it at his back. He shall do work for the king for one full month" (Kriwaczek, 2010, p. 211).

Women of the palace were under even tighter regulation. The king's wives and concubines would be locked up for the entirety of their lives, with the only visitors allowed being eunuchs, and even then only for a very brief time. The palace commander would have to grant permission and wait outside the entrance of the women's quarters to escort the eunuch when he had finished his business. A eunuch who overheard women arguing or singing would have one of his ears removed and would be beaten. If he spoke to a woman for longer than deemed necessary, he would be flogged and have his clothes taken. Anybody who spoke to one of the palace women without a chaperone, or anyone who was aware of a breach in the protocol but failed to report it, would be killed.

In this, Assyria became the model for many future societies, including Persian, Byzantine, and Islamic. But why was it that women's role in society changed so dramatically and so quickly? The answer is somewhat surprising and relates to another significant change in culture from around this time, specifically that of religious practice.

As the Assyrians grew in strength, and as their political paranoia shaped them into the ruthless nation they are known for today, there was a profound shift in the way one thought about the gods. For millennia, gods had been part of the world, the embodiment of natural forces—the winds, the rain, famine, rivers. At this point in history, however, when the individual was being reshaped by Assyrian ideals, the connection between the gods and nature fractured. Over time, the representation of the gods grew distant from the real world, eventually leading to their replacement by symbols over characters—stars, the sun, the moon, leaves, water, and numerous other representations. As time passed, the gods became transcendent as opposed to imminent; once a part of nature, they were now detached from it, above it.

As humanity had been made by the gods and in their image, the human relationship with nature shattered as well. Once awed by natural forces, now men were the master of nature, given "dominion over the fish and the sea, and over the fowl of the air, and over the cattle, and over all the earth, and over every creeping thing that creepeth upon the earth" (Carroll & Prickett, 2008, Genesis 1:26).

It was not so simple for women, however. In a world of transcendent religion, any connection with biology was frowned upon, considered to be inhuman. Women, unlike men, are bound firmly to the biological world, and according to the Assyrians, it was this that dictated their purpose and usefulness in life. Childbirth and menstruation were symbolic of a woman's inferior nature. Women were nothing more than a danger to men's semi-divinity. This attitude would stick for centuries, with its consequences still felt today. Women were largely excluded from religion until the rise of Christianity and their belief in Jesus, the son of God, being born from a woman.

An additional consequence of this theological change was the development of the very first monotheistic religion. The idea of transcendent, omnipresent deities is only a small step away from a single overarching deity, and before long the Assyrians considered Ashur to be the one true god, all others to simply be elements or interpretations of him. Those gods worshipped by outsiders were found to be reinterpretations (or misinterpretations) of Ashur. This was not to imply that the worship of other gods ceased entirely, merely that it was now recognized that these other gods were parts of Ashur himself, one of his many facets. Whether the monotheism of the Abrahamic religions stemmed from this origin or developed independently is difficult to say for certain, but it can be said with some certainty that their idea of a singular, overarching god was by no means a new one.

The Military State

Semitic arrivals from the west were a part of Mesopotamian history since the beginning. The Akkadians joined the Sumerians in prehistoric times, followed by the Amorites, who established the Old Babylonian Empire. The Arameans in the Assyrian days were simply the next in a long tradition. The reasons for this mass migration remain unclear, but we can deduce that there had been a motivational push from their old homeland, likely in the form of drought and famine. The lands of Assyria were not unaffected, but they remained at least somewhat fertile, and the rainfall was greater than on the eastern Mediterranean coastline. The Arameans probably moved into Assyrian land out of mere necessity, and upon their arrival they plundered and seized land, causing havoc across the western Assyrian borders.

Faced with this mounting threat, the Assyrians realized their best hope at survival lay in the development of an incontestable military. The ultimate solution to the Aramean problem was to build up military strength (a multi-generational process) and seize the Semitic homelands, forcing the population to remain. This goal was the final piece in the puzzle that would lead to Assyrian supremacy across Mesopotamia.

The cost of holding new territory, however, must be funded by the looting of even more lands further outside borders. The Assyrians quickly came to realize that the construction of an empire was not a simple undertaking and that it would take on a life of its own, swallowing up new territories simply to fund those already conquered. By around the 10th century BCE, the Assyrians began to swallow up not only their lost lands but also the lands of their neighbors, consuming the Aramean kingdoms in the west. By the rule of Tiglath-Pileser III in the eighth century BCE, the Assyrians had created the largest empire yet known to humankind.

The key to their military success was their military might. The Assyrian army was the model from which all other armies were drawn right up until the invention of firearms. Where warfare had previously been unorganized, one chaotic mass fighting against another, the Assyrians were disciplined and efficient. They were the first fielded army to be equipped in iron, a far superior and cheaper metal than bronze, which had been the standard of the time. They were one of the earliest armies to employ horses not merely for the pulling of chariots, but for use as cavalry. Furthermore, they invented the military boot, replacing the sandal, which allowed them to fight on any terrain. Their armies had a highly developed command structure, which allowed discipline to be enforced. If one were to look out at an Assyrian army lined up before a city, they would see up to 50,000 armored men standing in perfect formation. The Assyrians, through several generations of hard work and social reform, had created a militarized state that would change the face of warfare forever.

They also knew how to use fear to conquer their enemies, and would proudly announce their most violent punishments in warning to others. One Assyrian king, quoted by Mark (2014), described in great and gory detail the punishments inflicted upon chieftains who had revolted during his reign:

I built a pillar over against the city gate and I flayed all the chiefs who had revolted and I covered the pillar with their skins. Some I impaled upon the pillar on stakes and others I bound to stakes round the pillar... I made one pillar of the living and another of heads and I bound their heads to tree trunks round about the city. Their young men and maidens I consumed with fire. The rest of their warriors I consumed with thirst in the desert of the Euphrates. (para. 6)

Assyrian military conquests were focused on the capture of locations that either posed a threat or represented great strategic importance. Trade routes and towns were captured and held, as were the larger of Assyria's neighbors, while those who appeared to be insignificant were largely left to their own devices. As a result, the empire began to take on an unusual shape, with pockets of independence within its perceived borders. That said, while the Assyrians allowed some nations to retain their independence (within reason), should a state rise against them, they would wipe out the rebellious forces and annex the state immediately. Over time, more and more independent kingdoms were brought into the fold, plugging up the gaps within the Assyrian borders.

At its apex, the Assyrian Empire covered an enormous area of land stretching across the entirety of the Near East and even down into Egypt. Every free inhabitant within its borders was considered a free Assyrian citizen, for military might can only hold territory for a limited time. There was a firm ideology rooted in the Assyrian imperial structure, one that has remained largely unchanged throughout the millennia and to the empires of the 19th and early 20th centuries. This ideology, while not as extreme and brittle as that of the Neo-Sumerians, was strong enough to bind people together for many hundreds of years.

All Assyrian territory was part of Assyria. There was no differentiation between the original Assyrian lands and those conquered in Egypt or the south. This was important because it avoided a hierarchy based upon location, and decreased the chances of those in the provinces, far from the seat of power, feeling out of place and rising up against the imperial forces. In older empires, where individuals retained their own culture and ethnic identity, organized resistance was common and occurred whenever there had been a perceived weakness at the center of power. By treating all lands (perhaps aside from the city of Ashur) the same, the Assyrians were able to decrease the chance of rebellions and dissatisfaction.

All people were subject to the same laws, the same taxation, the same burdens, and the same rewards. This avoided a divide between the native Assyrian population and the conquered people, the "us-and-them" perspective, which would have encouraged organized resistance.

Whether an individual was born in Ashur or born in Israel, in Babylon, or in Egypt, they were the same before the eyes of Ashur and before the king. To enforce this, many people from conquered territories were relocated across the empire, dispersed to new locations to separate them from their cultural identity. Over time, this would destroy their old identity and replace it with exclusive loyalty to Assyria.

The final piece of the Assyrian ideological web was the figurehead of the empire—both the ruler, the Assyrian emperor in Ashur, the empire personified; and the single god, Ashur, who existed within and behind all the primitive gods worshipped by newly conquered subjects and was accepted as the ultimate creator of all things—the Jehovah of the Assyrians.

This was the formula for an immensely powerful, long-lasting empire. However, as with all things of this scale, it had its flaws. The equality among all citizens of Assyria and the dispersion of people across the land would eventually lead to an imbalance in ethnicity. The immense influx of Arameans from the west, and the conquest of their cities and nations, led to the native Assyrians becoming a minority within their own empire. The Akkadian language was lost to all but the scholars, replaced by Aramaic, which would remain in use until being supplanted by Arabic in the seventh century. As such, this imperial principle of inclusion and equality would spell the end of a culture, or at the very least a millennia-old linguistic tradition, built upon the Sumerian and Akkadian languages. Mesopotamia had conquered the world (or a significant part of it), yet the world had then conquered Mesopotamia.

Chapter 6: The End of an Era (After ca. 700 BCE)

The Decline of Culture

When one thinks of the fall of civilization, what most likely comes to mind is dramatic conquests, vicious battles, and crumbling cities. We tend to think of empires swallowed up, piece by piece, or even a foreign usurper taking up the mantle of power and enforcing their cultural practices upon the people of the city. After all, this is how Byzantine culture fell, and Roman, and countless others. In the case of the Assyrians, however, and the Mesopotamian tradition as a whole, the cause was something far more unusual—an alphabet.

To blame the fall of Mesopotamian culture on nothing but an alphabet may be an overstatement, but the introduction of a syllabic writing system was one of the largest contributors to the erasure of thousands of years of culture and tradition. Culture is, after all, rooted in language. A language combines and interprets common experiences and histories, creating terminology specific to one particular way of seeing the world. Our understanding of the world is limited by the language we can use to describe it, and as such the loss of a language means in turn the loss of a certain perspective, a way of understanding the world.

The mass migration eastward of the Aramean people would spell the end of Mesopotamian culture more completely than any military conquest ever could. The dispersal of Arameans throughout the empire, growing to become the majority in most areas, led in turn to the abandonment of both Sumerian and Akkadian as the imperial tongue. Even worse, however, was the invention of a syllabic alphabet, an entirely new way of recording information. This invention was not only going to eradicate a culture but also condemn information and accounts from the late Assyrian period largely to the dust.

The new alphabet had been developed for common people, designed with symbols representative of specific sounds to make the formation of words easy for even those with lesser education. This first alphabet, designed for use with the Aramaic language and not the Akkadian of the empire, was so easy to learn and use that it encouraged the adoption of Aramaic empire-wide. To make matters worse, the Aramaic alphabet was written using inks on papyrus or animal skins, biodegradable materials that would rarely last longer than a century or two before rotting away to nothing. The quick adoption of this new form of writing, and the language which it was designed for, resulted in a dramatic decrease in the number of cuneiform tablets produced and thus preserved from this era. As a result, much information is lost to the dark recesses of history, and what we do know either comes from the rare uncovering of a cuneiform tablet or the writings of those who came later, tending toward bias and incorrect information.

While it is difficult to make many bold statements about the late Assyrian period, we have evidence to suggest the Assyrians were aware of their impending fate and were making efforts to preserve their culture while they had the chance. Ashurbanipal, king of Assyria from 669-631 BCE, during which time he ruled from his capital, Nineveh, is considered the last great king of Assyria. During his reign, Ashurbanipal set about creating a collection of writings from across his empire, including Sumerian, Akkadian, Babylonian, and Assyrian cuneiform tablets, storing them in his library in Nineveh—perhaps the first organized library in history.

What is of interest here is not so much the collection itself, but the urgency with which Ashurbanipal set about compiling it. He collected tens of thousands of tablets, including religious texts, stories, and handbooks, and was constantly on the lookout for new additions. Kriwaczek (2010) quotes a letter he sent to a city governor requesting documents:

You shall search for and send to me... rituals, prayers, stone inscriptions, and whatever is useful to royalty such as expiation texts for cities, to ward off the evil eye at a time of panic, and whatever else is required in the palace, all that is available, and also rare tablets of which no copies exist in Assyria. (p. 234)

Ashurbanipal's timing could not have been more prudent. In the year 612 BCE, the city of Nineveh was sacked and destroyed by a joint force of Babylonians, Medians, and Scythians, sealing the fate of the Assyrian Empire. The penultimate king of Assyria, Sinsharishkun, was killed in the battle, and the library was destroyed. Thankfully, due to the hardy nature of clay tablets, the destruction of Nineveh resulted in the preservation of Ashurbanipal's collection under the rock until it was rediscovered in the 1800s. Ashurbanipal's hope of preserving his nation's culture and knowledge for future generations had succeeded, after more than 2,500 years.

The Decline of Power

The destruction of Nineveh, alongside that of Ashur, spelled the end of the Assyrian empire after long years of conflict with Babylon. Babylon had held a complicated position in Assyrian history, largely due to the cultural debt owed by the Assyrians to the Old Babylonian empire. During most of the Assyrian Empire's rule, Babylon was held under its sway, but there remained a king in Babylon, often assigned by the ruler of Assyria himself. The fall of Assyria was an unfortunate side effect of the long-standing imperial attitude toward their neighbors and client states— "It was the almost inevitable consequence of the imperial policy of *Oderint dum Metuant*, let them hate so long as they fear. For when the fear is overcome, the hatred remains" (Kriwaczek, 2010, p. 237).

The fall of Nineveh was so complete that, according to the Greek writer Lucian, there was "no trace of it left, and one can't even guess where it was" (Vlaardingerbroek, 2004, p. 233). This was not quite the end of the Mesopotamian story, however. There would be one final power in the land, ruling for no longer than the Soviet Union held power in the 1900s.

The Neo-Babylonian Empire, sometimes referred to as the Second Babylonian Empire, remerged from the sacking of Ashur and Nineveh around 612 BCE. Following the death of Ashurbanipal, the Babylonians had revolted against the new Assyrian kings, who had proven weaker and incapable of holding on to their territory in a changing age. The Neo-Babylonian Empire represented the first time in more than a millennium that Babylon had been the seat of power in Mesopotamia. The empire itself only lasted until around 539 BCE, and it ruled over the end of an era.

There was an increasing awareness among the people of Mesopotamia that the world as they knew it was coming to an end. Kabiti-Ilani-Marduk wrote a text during the last days of the Neo-Babylonians, known as *The Myth of the Pest-God Irra, The King of All Habitations,* that tells of the impending fall of Mesopotamian civilization. He tells of the plague-god, Irra, persuading the gods to allow him to lay waste to the lands of Sumer and of Akkad. His alleged motivation is the lack of piety among the people, a common explanation offered for the waning of empires and reminiscent of the attitudes following the fall of Akkad.

According to Kabiti-Ilani-Marduk, however, this was not the end. The actions of Irra were not intended merely to destroy the world and its people; rather, they were to clear away the old and make room for a new era. It is representative of the age-old idea, whereby destruction of the old is necessary for progress; that destruction is the ultimate creative force behind history.

In 549 BCE, the Median Empire, which stretched across modern-day Iran and up into Anatolia, was conquered by Cyrus the Great of Persia. Cyrus was considered by many to be a reasonable ruler, and the Persians were known for letting their subjects rule themselves as long as their kings paid homage to Cyrus and his successors, the King of Kings, ruling from Persepolis. Following the fall of Medes, it was inevitable that Babylon would follow, and in 539 BCE, this inevitability became reality. Babylon was attacked during a festival day when the populace was unprepared to defend the city. They opened the sluices and lowered the river, marched across, and occupied the city with relative ease. According to Herodotus (2015):

...if the Babylonians had only been given forewarning of what Cyrus was up to, or fathomed it for themselves, then they could have turned the entrance of the Persians into their city so completely to their own advantage as to have annihilated the invaders utterly... However, the enemy was upon them before they knew what had hit them... Such was the size of the city that those who lived in the centre of Babylon had no idea that the suburbs had fallen. (p. 191)

Babylon fell to the Persians; the age of Mesopotamia had come to a close.

There are multiple accounts of how the Persians may have been received by the Babylonians. According to some, they were caught unawares and thus had no option but to surrender, but others suggest the Babylonians welcomed Persian rule with open arms. It was agreed that Cyrus was a worthy king, and the previous ruler of Babylon had not been well-loved. An unearthed tablet from around the time, however, shows a receipt for 7 weeks worth of work on one of the city walls, suggesting that perhaps the conquest was not so easy as it may have been implied by later sources.

It was believed by the Babylonians that the conquest of Persia would not spell the end of their culture. After all, many outsiders had entered the land between the two rivers in the past and set themselves up as rulers, adopting local customs themselves. It was most likely assumed by many that this would be no different, particularly considering their culture was the oldest and most respected in the region.

This belief was terribly mistaken. While Cyrus and his successors adopted elements of Mesopotamian culture for their own, this was no different from the open attitude displayed to all conquered nations. Persia was built upon a selection of cultural practices taken from all their conquered states and kingdoms, and Mesopotamia was no more or less important than the others. Furthermore, unlike earlier conquerors and invaders, the kings of Persia chose not to rule from one of the great Mediterranean cities but remained in Persepolis. Rule from the outside would remain for millennia. The consequences of this were immense. Mesopotamia, once the cultural beacon of the east, had lost both its self-confidence and centrality, reduced to a mere province. This was not effective immediately, of course—cultures do not die out overnight, rather wither away slowly, almost unnoticed, supplanted by more modern practices.

The rise of Persia represented not so much a new age, but more a period of transition. The world was now opened up to new ideas, peoples, and cultures—a sign of things to come. The true transition into a new era occurred when Alexander the Macedonian, ruler of the first great western power, rolled his war machine eastward and burnt Persepolis to ashes in 330 BCE. This Hellenistic era, with Greek ideas and practices spreading from Italy to India and beyond, was the beginning of the modern age, the new world in which we ourselves live. But Mesopotamia, the colossus of the ancient past, had by this time shriveled and collapsed, buried under the rubble of a bygone age.

Part 2:

The Mythology

Chapter 7: Enuma Elish

The Enuma Elish (meaning "when on high," taken from the opening lines) is a Babylonian creation myth telling of Marduk, the champion of the gods, and his victory over the forces of Tiamat. Being of Babylonian origin, it is believed that the original story from which this is derived will have featured either Enki or Enlil in the major role. It appears to have been told in such a way to justify the reign of Marduk, the Babylonian supreme god, over all the previous deities of Sumer and Akkad. Tablets telling this story have been found in the excavation of Ashur, Kish, and the Library of Ashurbanipal in Nineveh, and date to ca. 1200 BCE, although the original myth is believed to be much older.

In the beginning, there is water, and that water is swirling in chaos. The water parts into two distinct entities—the god Apsu, freshwater; and the goddess Tiamat, saltwater. Upon their separation, the two deities come together, mixing their waters to create a new generation of gods.

However, the young gods are loud and irritating, as children tend to be. Apsu, their great father, finds it difficult to sleep during the night, and even more difficult to work during the day. On the suggestion of his vizier Mummu, Apsu does what any loving father would in such a situation: he decides to have them killed.

Tiamat, aware of her husband's intentions, is rightfully upset at the idea of her children being murdered. They are loud and obnoxious, but they are also young, and she had brought them into the world—she is duty-bound to protect them. As such, Tiamat seeks Enki, her great-grandson, and tells him of his father's terrible plan.

Enki is shocked. The other gods, upon being told of their father's murderous intentions, are similarly taken aback, uncertain of how to act. After a good deal of contemplation, Enki comes up with a masterful plan.

Late one night, he sneaks into Apsu's abode and pours sleep upon him. Mummu, who tries to wake Apsu and warn him, is instead captured and chained up. With his father incapacitated, Enki removes his crown and places it upon his own head, before slaying Apsu where he lies.

In a stroke of genius, Enki decides to create a dwelling for himself and his fellow younger gods within the corpse of their father. In the subsequent excitement and celebration, Enki and his wife Damkina come together and bear a son, Marduk, whose greatness and splendor exceeds even the greatest among the younger gods.

Meanwhile, Tiamat grieves the loss of her husband. She may have warned Enki of Apsu's plans in the first place, but she had never intended to simply swap out one death for another. In her grief, Tiamat gathers an assembly of great allies, with her son Kingu at its head. She creates 11 terrible chimeras, horrendous, disgusting monsters the likes of which the world had never before seen, and bestows upon Kingu the Tablets of Destiny, legitimizing his rule over the entire universe. Her army assembled, Tiamat declares war upon the younger gods, seeking terrible vengeance for the death of her first husband, Apsu.

The war does not go well for the younger gods. Many fearsome battles ensue, and there are numerous turncoats, gods who abandon Enki and instead support Tiamat. With her great army and her 11 monsters, Tiamat is believed to be invincible.

Enki, fearing for the worst, speaks to his grandfather, Tiamat's son Anshar. He tells Anshar of their terrible odds, and of Kingu, wielding the Tablet of Destinies, leading the 11 monsters into battle. Anshar, concerned, seeks out his son, Enki's father Anu, and asks him to go to Tiamat and to appease her. Anu sets off, but the closer he comes to Tiamat, the greater his fear. In a moment of weakness, Anu turns back, returning to his father in shame.

The younger gods are running out of options quickly. In a desperate last attempt, Anshar suggests Marduk, son of Enki, serve as their champion. Marduk is brought before them and he asks which god he will be fighting.

"You will fight no god," they tell Marduk. "You will be fighting the goddess, Tiamat."

Marduk, apparently feeling confident, declares that he will fight and defeat the goddess Tiamat, but only on one condition—upon his victory, he is to be proclaimed the supreme god, ruler over even Enki, Anu, and Anshar. The younger gods have little choice—they must either accept Marduk's terms, or submit to the murderous wrath of Tiamat. In the end, there is no decision to be made at all. Even Lahmu and Lahamu, Tiamat's firstborn children, are eventually convinced of Marduk's worthiness, although not without first drinking themselves into a stupor. Marduk will be the supreme god.

The younger gods provide Marduk with a throne that sat above all other gods. They make him a scepter and provide him with a wide array of weapons with which to fight Tiamat—a bow and quiver, a mace, bolts of lightning, and four winds. The gods kneel before him, proclaiming "Lord Marduk, your word is the first among all gods. If you command destruction, it shall be so; if you command creation, it shall be so."

Marduk, proclaimed supreme god and equipped with every weapon he could want for, sets out to capture and slay his great-great-grandmother, Tiamat. Using the four winds, he traps her, and then approaches in a chariot, condemning her for the trouble she had created. Enraged at such treatment, Tiamat makes the mistake of joining Marduk in single combat.

Marduk throws a net over Tiamat, and try as she may, she is unable to escape. In her rage, she opens her mouth to swallow Marduk whole, but instead, he fills her mouth with the *Imhullu*, the evil wind. Dazed and confused, the evil wind raging inside her, Tiamat becomes incapacitated and Marduk takes the opportunity to fire an arrow into her heart. Tiamat, the mother of all gods, is slain.

In one last act of defiance, he smashes Tiamat's head in with a mace, and from her crushed eyes flowed the waters of the Euphrates and the Tigris rivers. Splitting his mother's corpse in two, Marduk creates the sky from one half, the earth from the other, and in the skies creates a place for himself, his grandfather Anu, his father Enki, and Enlil.

As the supreme god, Marduk sets about putting his realm in order. He creates constellations and uses them to define the days of the year. He creates the moon, weather, and the day and night cycle. Finally, he seeks to create humankind, subjects, and servants for the gods. Consulting his father, it was decided that a god must be sacrificed from whose blood humans would be created. It did not take long for them to settle on a suitable candidate—Kingu, who had remained under lock and key since Tiamat's defeat.

In one last major act, Marduk divides the gods into two realms—those who will reside in the heavens, and those who will reside on the earth, thus arranging the pantheon and his realm. The gods, in honor of Marduk, decide to construct him a shrine; he instead tells them to construct the great city of Babylon. In the city, the gods build the *Esagila*, the Temple to Marduk, and make it an earthly abode for Marduk, Enki, and Enlil.

Chapter 8: The Myth of Adapa

The Myth of Adapa is the Mesopotamian myth explaining why humans are mortal. It tells of Adapa, the first man created by Enki, being tricked into declining the gift of immortality. A comparison can be made to the story of Adam and Eve in Genesis when Yahweh banished the pair before they could eat from the Tree of Life. The myth is believed to have originated in the Babylonian Kassite period, and was retold in the third century BCE by Berossus, who used the name Oannes in place of Adapa.

Adapa, the first man created by Enki, the god of wisdom, is a man of many qualities. The great god has seen fit to endow him with great wisdom and intelligence, strength, and bravery, and yet has left him mortal.

One day, Adapa is fishing in the gulf when a strong southerly wind caused his boat to capsize. Adapa is hurled into the ocean, and, spluttering and choking on the salty water, rages at the south wind, breaking its wings so that it can no longer blow. Anu, the sky god, is furious and sends for Adapa, demanding the man explain himself.

Before heading to confront Anu, Adapa is taken aside by Enki, who counsels him on how to behave before the gods. Enki was the father of men, and as such, Adapa trusted him more than any other, listening intently to Enki's advice.

"Firstly," Enki tells him, "you must flatter Tammuz and Gishida, the guardians at the gates. Tell them you remember them from another time, that you are familiar with their names and importance. This will please the guardians, and they will speak favorably of you to great Anu.

"When you come into the presence of Anu, you must refuse all food and drink you are offered. The food that Anu offers you will be the food of death, a punishment for your transgressions against the south wind. That said, you must accept any oil to anoint yourself with, and any clothing that is offered to you."

Adapa is sure to do exactly what Enki tells him. He honors both Tammuz and Gishida respectfully at the door, and, while anointing himself and accepting a robe, declines all food he is offered. Anu asks him to explain his actions, and Adapa does, admitting he acted rashly and out of anger.

However, Adapa does not realize he has been tricked; for Enki feared that Anu may offer Adapa the food of eternal life, and having made Adapa wise and brave already, had to ensure his creation remained tethered somehow, unable to rise and challenge him. As such, Enki had deceived Adapa, convincing him to decline the food he was offered, and as such ensuring that humans would never gain immortality. Anu, perplexed by Adapa's refusal to eat the food of life, sends the man back to earth to live out his life as a mortal.

Anu meant no harm to Adapa, and in his offering of the food to Adapa, had been attempting to find a solution to one of the fundamental existential questions of life: if you are born only to die, and you live knowing you will soon die, what point is there to living? The remainder of this tale is too damaged to recount, but it appears that Anu, Enki's father, summons his son and chastises him for deceiving Adapa and preventing him from tasting the food of life.

Chapter 9: The Myth of Etana

According to the Sumerian King List, Etana reigned as the king of Kish early in the third millennium BCE. Etana was a well-known and respected individual and was likely chosen as the main character of this myth for that very reason. The myth's central message is one of piety, of loving, and of obeying the gods. While the date of composition is unknown, the British Museum holds fragments of the myth dated from Ashurbanipal's Library, almost certainly a late copy of the original story.

Shortly following the emergence of order from chaos, and the birth of humanity, the gods created the great city of Kish. Having built magnificent walls to protect the inhabitants of the city from the dangers outside, the gods select a king from among the people. Etana is chosen as king by the goddess Ishtar, and he immediately sets about building a shrine to the god Adad.

Beside the shrine, there grows a poplar, and within the poplar tree, an eagle and a snake make their homes. The two creatures both swear an oath of loyalty before the sun god, Shamash, promising to watch over one another, to watch over the other's children. This is a fruitful arrangement, and both the eagle and the serpent live in comfort and happiness until, one day, while the snake is out looking for food, the eagle consumes his children, breaking his oath.

The snake returns home from his hunt to find his nest destroyed and his children gone. Around the nest, the footprints and feathers of an eagle lie scattered, and the snake makes the obvious conclusion. Lifting his head to the sky, he calls to the sun god, crying out for justice.

Shamash, far above, takes pity on the snake. He tells the snake to hide inside the carcass of a wild beast and wait for the eagle to arrive to feed. When the eagle arrives, the snake is instructed to seize him, pluck his features, sever his wings, and toss him into a pit. The snake does as Shamash instructs, and soon the eagle lies broken at the bottom of the pit, punished for the breaking of his oath sworn before the sun god.

At the bottom of the pit, the eagle looks up to the sky and cries out to Shamash. Shamash looks down upon the eagle with pity, and he tells the eagle, "what you did was a terrible thing. You broke your word, a sacred oath sworn before me.

But I will have mercy on you, and I will send Etana, the king of Kish, to help you."

It is no coincidence that Etana himself was, at that very moment, also petitioning Shamash. Etana had learned his wife was barren, and he feared dying without an heir to the throne. Shamash tells Etana to go to the pit and rescue the eagle. Upon retrieving the eagle, Etana nurses the bird back to health, and the two grow close.

While Etana nurses him back to health, the eagle repays the king's kindness by interpreting his dreams. In one dream, Etana ascends to the heavens riding upon an eagle and is offered the plant of birth by Ishtar, who had been the one to select him as king. The eagle concludes that this dream is a message, an instruction for them to attempt this very journey. His wings stronger, and his feathers having grown back, the eagle carries Etana into the sky.

Clutching tightly to the underbelly of the eagle, Etana is carried so high that when he looks down, he can no longer see the city, or in fact the entire earth. Etana grows afraid, and cries out to the eagle: "I cannot see the land, nor can I see the sea! We are up so high! Please, my friend, I do not want to go to heaven. Return me to my city!" Etana, so desperate to return to the safety of solid ground, lets go of the eagle and plummets. The eagle, shocked, dives after Etana and manages to catch him before he hits the earth. The two of them decide it is probably best if they return to the city.

Shortly after their return, both Etana and his wife begin to have similar dreams. The eagle, interpreting the dreams once again, tells Etana that the gods wish him to make a second attempt, to once again ascend heavenward. Harnessing every ounce of courage, Etana clings to the eagle, and they ascend, and this time they reach heaven without incident.

Unfortunately, the tablets we have uncovered are cut off at this point. It is understood, based on the Sumerian King List, that Etana had a son, Balikh, who succeeded him and reigned for 1,500 years. As a result, it is fair to assume they were greeted warmly by the gods, and that Ishtar gifted Etana the Plant of Birth, with which he and his wife were able to conceive a son.

Chapter 10: The Atrahasis Myth

The Atrahasis Myth tells of the great flood unleashed upon the earth by the gods. The story itself is very similar to the flood story in the Epic of Gilgamesh, only in this edition it is not Utnapishtim, but Atrahasis, who builds the ark. It is also almost identical to an older story, the Eridu Genesis, of which we have only uncovered fragments. In real life, the flood itself was likely caused by natural, local events, but the tale shows it being of epic proportions. The Atrahasis Myth was likely written sometime in the 17th century BCE, during the reign of Hammurabi's great-grandson Ammi-Saduqa.

Following the creation of the earth, but before the first human beings, the gods work on the land, digging out the Euphrates and Tigris river beds, laying the foundations for cities. However, the younger of the gods begin to rebel against this intense labor, and so Enki, the god of wisdom, decides to create a new race of creatures who will do the work for them. The god We-Ilu offers himself up as a sacrifice, and the goddess Nintu mixes his body and mind with clay to create seven male and seven female humans.

The creation of humanity is a huge relief to the gods, who no longer need to labor long hours, leaving the work instead to their new servants. In time, however, the people grow too loud, always shouting and fighting and singing, preventing the gods from sleeping. Enlil, the supreme god, finds it particularly irritating, and decides something must be done.

Looking down at their creation, the gods consider what to do. The humans had clearly been of great use, but it was clear now that their creation had been a mistake. Enlil proposes a cull, lowering the population below by unleashing drought, disease, and famine upon the earth.

This does not have the desired effect. Instead of lessening their noise, the disasters sent by Enlil only serve to make the humans louder. They cry up to the gods, and to Enki in particular, to relieve their suffering. Enki offers guidance, but Enlil's patience has worn thin, and so he persuades the other gods to join him in summoning a terrible flood to wipe humanity from the earth.

Enki looks down at the humans, his creation, and feels pity for them. He knows he cannot save them all, so he descends to the earth and warns

Atrahasis, a kind, loyal, and wise man, of the impending flood.

"Build an enormous ark," he tells Atrahasis, "and within it, bring two of every animal. Only this way will life be preserved."

Atrahasis does as he is bid, and no sooner than he completes his work, the great clouds gather in the sky, and the deluge pours across the land. The storm is terrible, and even the gods are afraid, and they weep as they look down upon the terrible destruction and suffering. As the sky clears, even Enlil, who had proposed the flood, realizes his mistake. He is repentant, wishing he had never brought such a terrible catastrophe upon the people below. He knows, however, that what is done is done, and that there is no way to undo it.

It is at this point that Atrahasis, far below, finds land and opens his ark. Having witnessed such a humbling ordeal, and eternally grateful to the gods for his family's survival, he immediately sends up a sacrifice to the heavens. Enlil is caught off guard, confused as to how there could be sacrifices still ascending even after he had just killed off all the humans.

Enki comes forth and explains himself before the gods. At first, Enlil is furious, and despite his prior regret, he berates Enki for going behind his back. Enki proposes a new solution to the problem, however, one that will prevent the population of humans from ever growing too great again.

"We will create new humans," he says, "humans that are not as fertile as the last. We can prevent them from overpopulating by creating women who cannot bear children, others who will remain virgins and spend their lives in the temples. We will bring forth demons who will steal infants away, who will cause miscarriages. This way, we will never need to worry about the humans growing too noisy, and we can live our lives in peace."

The gods all agree that this is a fantastic plan, and so set about creating their new race of humans. The new humans populate the world below, inhabiting the ruins of the cities and building them up to their former glory. Atrahasis, however, is taken by the gods and lifted away to a new paradise, far from the new race of humans, where he lives in peace and comfort for eternity.

Chapter 11: The Epic of Gilgamesh

The Epic of Gilgamesh is the best-known ancient Mesopotamian epic and tells the story of the mythical king of Uruk, Gilgamesh, and his quest for immortality. The tale was no doubt shared orally at first, and as a result, it is difficult to date the original work. That said, numerous copies have been unearthed over the last two centuries, with the most complete version being told over 12 clay tablets and dating from around the 12-10th century BCE. The original epic is told over about 1,950 lines.

Gilgamesh, king of the city of Uruk, is a man of the greatest wisdom, bravery, and strength. One-third human, two-thirds god, Gilgamesh constructed the great walls of his city to keep enemies and invaders out, and to protect his people from any threat. There is, however, one threat he is unable to protect them from—himself.

Despite his great qualities, Gilgamesh is an oppressive ruler. He exhausts the men of the city through tests of strength and forced labor, but the greatest of his crimes was that of the "lord's right" to sleep with brides on their wedding nights, a right that Gilgamesh enjoys to the detriment of his people. Upset and angry, his people cry out to the gods, desperate for release from their king's oppressive reign. Upon hearing the pleas of the Urukian people, the gods decide to create a man equal and yet opposite to Gilgamesh, to balance out his strength and put him in his place. The man they create is Enkidu, a 'wild-man' who lives out in the forests among the beasts, attacking shepherds and eating their sheep. The people of Uruk suffer as Enkidu consumes their livestock, uproots their game traps, and ruins their fields.

A plan is devised by which Enkidu could be tamed, transformed into a civilized man. A temple prostitute, Shamhat, is sent beyond the walls of Uruk to track down Enkidu and to tame him, for it was known that upon union with the temple prostitute, Enkidu will lose his wild nature and instead learn the ways of civilization. Shamhat finds Enkidu and seduces him, and after laying together for six days and seven nights, Enkidu discovers that the animals of the forest find his new behaviors to be strange and shun him. Shamhat teaches him the common practices of civilization, and together the two of them return to the city of Uruk.

Upon their return to the city, Shamhat and Enkidu find Gilgamesh attending a wedding. It is, of course, Gilgamesh's right to bed the bride on her wedding night, and he had come for this very purpose. Upon learning of Gilgamesh's intentions, Enkidu is disgusted, demanding Gilgamesh forfeit his right to the bride. He blocks the bedchamber entrance and challenges Gilgamesh to a duel. Should Gilgamesh make it past Enkidu, he could enter the chamber and claim the woman; however, if Enkidu should defeat him, Gilgamesh must forfeit his right to new brides.

Gilgamesh accepts the challenge, and the two of them fight late into the night until eventually, Gilgamesh overcomes his rival, and Enkidu concedes. Despite his victory, Gilgamesh spares Enkidu's life and honors his wishes, forfeiting the right to sleep with the bride. They return to the palace as friends, and Gilgamesh follows Enkidu's lead by learning the virtues of mercy and humility, working hard to be a more reasonable ruler for his people. In time, the two of them grow very close, becoming almost inseparable.

Many years pass and Gilgamesh grows bored and lazy. Seeking new adventures, he suggests the two of them should travel to the Cedar Forest and defeat the great beast, Humbaba. Humbaba is said to be part demon, part ogre, and is the protector of the Cedar Forest. While Enkidu objects to the plan at first, he finds it is impossible to change Gilgamesh's mind and eventually agrees to join him on the adventure.

The two of them set off across the desert, but each night Gilgamesh finds himself experiencing terrible nightmares. In one, he sees Enkidu lying still on a bed, unmoving; in another, he sees a giant stone monster, clasping Gilgamesh around the waist, squeezing him. Gilgamesh confides in Enkidu, who offers encouragement, assuring him that the dreams are merely signs of their victory. It means that they will return home safely, he explains, and that Gilgamesh's legacy will be lifted to the heavens.

Arriving at the Cedar Forest, Enkidu and Gilgamesh proceed to cut down the surrounding trees. The loud sound of falling trees quickly attracts the attention of Humbaba, who attacks the two men. A great battle ensues, during which Gilgamesh bribes the creature, offering his sisters to Humbaba as wives, in an attempt to trick Humbaba into giving up its layers of armor. Finally, Gilgamesh is victorious. The monster, clinging to life, begs mercy of Gilgamesh, who falters, uncertain of how to proceed. Seeing

Gilgamesh's uncertainty, Humbaba takes the chance to curse the two men, and so Gilgamesh kills it.

The two men cut down the tallest tree of the forest, and from it, they construct a magnificent gate to set in the walls of Uruk. Cutting down several other trees, they lash the trunks together to form a raft and use it to carry their great gate downriver toward Uruk.

Upon their return, Ishtar, goddess of love and war, daughter of the sky god Anu, expresses sexual desire for Gilgamesh, but Gilgamesh rejects her advances. Ishtar is taken aback, upset, and offended, and so convinces her father to send the Bull of Heaven down the Uruk to punish Gilgamesh for shaming her. With the Bull comes great plague, a famine which sweeps across the land, and terrible drought. Enkidu and Gilgamesh, worried for their people, fight and slay the bull, offering its heart to the god Shamash, and bringing the plague and drought to an end.

As the city celebrates the great victory of their ruler and his right-hand man, Enkidu falls unwell and begins to suffer from nightmares, not unlike Gilgamesh had done on their way to the Cedar Forest. In the nightmares, the gods curse Enkidu for the killing of the Bull and Humbaba, the demon-ogre of the forest. Enkidu, afraid, curses the day he met Shamhat, wishing he had instead remained in the forest, where he could have avoided the curse of the gods.

As he dies, Gilgamesh remains beside his bed, watching over him. He listens as Enkidu tells him of the House of Dust, the underworld where the dead are clad in feathers, eat stone, and where no light ever shines. He tells of the skulls of kings in enormous piles. Upon his death, Enkidu leaves Gilgamesh terrified and distraught. Gilgamesh, deep in mourning, begs the gods to allow him to walk beside Enkidu in the afterlife. He stays beside the corpse, unmoving, wretched, until Enkidu's body begins to decay and has to be taken away.

Without his friend, Gilgamesh falls into depression, terrified of the afterlife Enkidu had described as he died. He vows to never enter the House of Dust, and so sets out to find Utnapishtim and his wife, the only humans ever granted immortality by the gods.

Gilgamesh sets out from Uruk, battling great monsters and overcoming terrible odds, and eventually reaches Mt. Mashu, the twin peaks at the end of the earth, where he finds the path blocked by two great scorpions. They laugh at Gilgamesh, telling him he cannot hope to achieve his goal and that immortality is impossible, but he convinces them of his desperation, and so they let him pass regardless. Gilgamesh continues beyond the mountain to a great tunnel through which the sun travels at the end of each day. Entering the tunnel, Gilgamesh treks for 12 leagues before finally emerging in a beautiful paradise.

As he wanders through the paradise, taking in the sights, Gilgamesh stumbles upon the wine-maker Siduri. Siduri, seeing his disheveled appearance, mistakes him for a murderer or a thief, but Gilgamesh manages to explain himself, and she directs him to the ferryman, Urshanabi, though not without first reminding him of the pointlessness of his quest.

Upon reaching the water's edge, Gilgamesh finds his way blocked by two great stone monsters. Believing them to be a threat, he fights and slays them both. At this point, Urshanabi arrives, and informs Gilgamesh he has made a terrible mistake—the stone creatures he killed were the only beings in existence who could help them cross the Waters of Death, beyond which he would find Utnapishtim. To pass, Urshanabi tells him, he will need to cut down 120 trees and shape them into punting poles, for as each touches the water, it will dissolve.

Gilgamesh sets to work and has soon fashioned 120 trees into the poles required for the crossing. They set out, traveling through a thick, dark mist, and eventually arrive at a small island whereupon Utnapishtim and his wife live.

Gilgamesh drops to his knees before Utnapishtim and recounts his story, begging for his help in achieving immortality. Utnapishtim admonishes Gilgamesh, telling him that immortality would do little more than wiping the joy from one's life, that the inevitability of death was what gave life purpose and meaning. Gilgamesh, not to be put off, asks Utnapishtim how he gained immortality, and Utnapishtim tells Gilgamesh the story of the flood.

The gods had a secret council, he explains, and decided to send a terrible flood to earth to wipe out humanity. Enki, however, feared for humanity and so snuck down to the earth and found Utnapishtim, telling him to build a boat, upon which he would take his entire family, his craftsmen, and all the animals he could find. Utnapishtim set to work, and had soon built an enormous ark, in which his family and animals resided as the storm approached. Even the gods cowered in fear as the great black clouds rolled across the land, and for six days and nights, a terrible storm ensued, with water pouring across the earth in great waves. The storm finally subsided, and the boat struck a mountain, becoming lodged in the rocks. Utnapishtim sent out birds, and when they failed to return, he opened the boat and released all the animals onto the land. He made a sacrifice to the gods, and Enlil, realizing there had been a survivor, was enraged. He descended to strike Utnapishtim down, but Enki and Ishtar intervened, condemning his terrible flood, and Enlil saw reason. He instead decided to bless Utnapishtim and his wife, as the first people of a new world, with immortality.

And so, Utnapishtim explains, immortality was a special, one-time gift. It was not something that could be accessible to anybody who desired it, and nor should it be, for it was no less a curse than a blessing.

Upon hearing this tale, Gilgamesh remains determined. Utnapishtim decides to test Gilgamesh's resolve and challenges the king to remain awake for six days and seven nights. Gilgamesh, however, falls asleep almost immediately, and Utnapishtim asks his wife to bake a loaf of bread for each day he sleeps. Upon waking, Gilgamesh denies having slept at all, but Utnapishtim shows him the loaves of bread, each in a different state of decay, and explains that one was baked on each day that he slept. Seeking to overcome death, Gilgamesh was unable even to overcome sleep.

Utnapishtim sends Gilgamesh back across the Waters of Death, and exiles Urshanabi alongside him. Just as they are parting, however, he takes pity on Gilgamesh and tells him of a plant in the deepest part of the ocean which, when one consumes it, will make him young once again. Intrigued, Gilgamesh travels to the ocean and ties rocks to his feet, descending to the depths in search of the plant. He finds it, and upon returning to the surface decides to test it on an old man when he returns to Uruk, so as not to unwittingly poison himself.

Unfortunately, as they travel toward the great city, Gilgamesh leaves the plant unguarded for a time and a snake consumes it. Gilgamesh finds the plant gone, and the snake has shed its skin, and so realizes that not only did the plant work but that he had just lost his one last chance at immortality. Weeping, he returns to Uruk with Urshanabi, and before its walls he drops to his knees, praising the immense walls of Uruk as his greatest achievement. He realizes, kneeling in the dust before his city, that eternal life is not a natural path for men, and that the walls, his greatest achievement, will stand for centuries after his death, thus preserving his name and legacy for eternity. It is not eternal life, he explains to Urshanabi, but eternal legacy, leaving a mark on the world, that grants a person true immortality.

It is here that the Epic of Gilgamesh ends, although in some cases a 12th tablet has been uncovered, apparently added at some point later and telling of events that appear to have no direct link to the original epic itself. In this additional tablet, Enkidu is once again alive, and Gilgamesh sends him down into the underworld to retrieve lost possessions. While in the underworld, Enkidu makes a series of mistakes that result in him being trapped, but Gilgamesh appeals to Enki and Shamash, who open up the earth and allow Enkidu to go free.

Chapter 12: The Descent of Inanna

The Descent of Inanna is a Sumerian poem, written sometime around 1900-1600 BCE. The story tells of Inanna, Queen of Heaven, traveling from the sky down into the underworld to visit Ereshkigal, her sister, whose husband had recently died. The story is one of injustice and the unfairness of life, with Inanna's bad choices leading to the suffering of others.

Inanna, clad in her finest clothes, the crown of heaven shining brightly upon her head, stands before the gates of the underworld. Pausing before she enters, she turns to her faithful servant Ninshubur, and imparts instructions on how to rescue her, should she fail to return. Ninshubur bows his head respectfully, and Inanna steps forward, knocking loudly on the ancient gates.

Behind the gates, Neti, the gatekeeper, appears and demands to know who seeks entrance to the underworld.

"It is I," she answers. "Inanna, Queen of Heaven."

Neti frowns.

"Why would you want to enter a land from which none return?"

"Because," she replies, "My sister Ereshkigal has been widowed. Her husband, Gugalanna, has died, and I have come for the funeral."

Neti asks Inanna to wait while he consults Ereshkigal. Upon learning of her sister's arrival, Ereshkigal seems uncomfortable, falling silent for a long time. Eventually, she tells Neti to bolt the seven gates dealing into the underworld, and then let Inanna in one gate at a time, removing a royal garment for each she passes.

Neti does as he is bid, and he allows Inanna to enter the underworld. At each gate, he requests she remove a garment or item. She first removes her crown, her beads, her ring, and her scepter. Even her clothing is removed, and by the time she enters the last gate, Inanna is entirely naked. She turns on Neti, demanding an explanation for this undignified treatment.

"Do not question the ways of the underworld," he replies. "They are perfect."

Inanna enters the throne room and bows before Ereshkigal, bare and humbled. As she approaches the throne to speak to her sister, the underworld's judges, the Annuna, quickly surround her, holding her in place. Together, they pass judgment upon Inanna, for it was she who caused the death of Gugalanna, the Bull of Heaven, for she had sent him down against the king of Uruk, Gilgamesh, after he had spurned her advances, and Gugalanna had been killed.

Ereshkigal bears down upon Inanna, cursing her for her selfishness, proclaiming her guilt. She strikes her sister, killing her, and mounts her corpse from a hook on the wall.

Meanwhile, Ninshubur had been waiting for his mistress to return. When three nights and three days have passed, Ninshubur ascends to heaven and seeks Enki, Inanna's father, begging for help. Enki, worried about his daughter, sends two *galla*, creatures neither male nor female, down into the earth to find Inanna. The two *galla* enter the underworld as if flies. As they approach Ereshkigal, the Queen of the Underworld begins to suffer greatly, experiencing pains as if in childbirth. The *galla* express their sympathy for her pain, and the Queen, grateful, offers them a gift of their choosing.

"We want nothing more than the corpse that hangs from the wall," they tell her, and she gives it to them willingly. The *galla*, having found

Inanna, resuscitate her with the food of life, and she rises from the dead.

Leaving the underworld, however, is not easily done. Having entered the realm of Ereshkigal, one can only depart if their place is taken by another. The *galla* ascend with Inanna and try to find a substitute for her, first seeking Ninshubur, and then her sons Shara and Lulal. Inanna, however, is having none of it, for Ninshubur and her sons are dressed in the clothing of mourning, believing her to be dead.

When she comes across Dumuzi, her lover, she finds him dressed in rich clothing and jewels. Inanna, hurt and angered that he is not mourning her as are the others, demands the *galla* seize him as her substitute in the underworld. Dumuzi, panic-stricken, appeals to the god Utu and is turned into a snake. He tries to slip away but is caught, and carried into the underworld to remain forever. Before he can arrive, however, the *galla* are stopped by his sister, Geshtinanna, who volunteers to share his fate, each spending half a year in the underworld and half a year in the heavens. It was by this bi-annual cycling that the seasons were created, as Geshtinanna was the goddess of agriculture and fertility, and could bless the earth for only half the year. Inanna, meanwhile, returned happily to her old life in the heavens, most probably unrepentant for the suffering she had inflicted upon those around her.

Chapter 13: The Curse of Agade

The Curse of Agade (Akkad) dates back to the Neo-Sumerian period and tells of the Akkadian king Naram-Sin and his confrontation with displeased gods. Naram-Sin was considered to be one of the greatest Akkadian rulers, and while the text appears to offer a mythological explanation for the collapse of Akkad and the empire, the king was likely chosen more for name recognition than because any of the events were true. If anything, it is probable that his successors were the true inspiration for the tale. The text focuses on the relationship between kings and gods, and warns about the consequences of impious behavior.

The great city of Akkad is the center of the world. Ruled by the magnificent Naram-Sin, the descendant of Sargon himself, the gates of Akkad are constantly flowing with wealth, taxes and tribute, gems and treasures. However, upon seeing the riches pouring into Akkad, the goddess Inanna (later Ishtar) feels that she and the other gods ought to be honored by those in the city—temples should be built, festivals held, sacrifices offered.

The supreme god Enlil does not agree. Enlil had destroyed Kish and placed the great Sargon on the throne of Akkad, leaving the goddess Inanna to watch over him and the city. However, now that Naram-Sin is king, Enlil is no longer pleased with the city, for what reasons, he will not say. He instructs the gods to withdraw from the city and no longer offer blessings to its inhabitants.

Naram-Sin, king of Akkad, dreams of a grim future for his city and empire. He sees cities burned to rubble, he sees floods and famine and invaders from outside lands. Naram-Sin decides to enter a period of mourning and prayer lasting seven years, waiting for the gods to offer counsel. However, no gods come to Naram-Sin, and, fearing for the future of his people and city, he decides he must do something to draw their attention.

Naram-Sin marches on the city of Ekur, the home of Enlil, and he puts the temple to the flame. The house of Enlil is turned to rubble, the inside on display for all to see. This act is the worst of transgressions, the greatest desecration possible. So great had been Naram-Sin's anger that he had turned to vandalizing the house of the supreme god. The other gods now come to Enlil's side—he may have been unreasonable before, but Naram-Sin's actions were unforgivable. The king had entered into a battle he could not possibly hope to win, and he was to suffer the greatest of punishments. As the empire is overrun by famine and foreign invaders, Enlil curses Akkad, driving out all who lived within its walls and leaving it barren. Naram-Sin had, at the cost of thousands of lives, learned his lesson—one must never turn his back on the gods.

Conclusion

On October 3rd, 1932, Iraq shed the chains of British rule and gained independence. While perhaps lost on many, the significance of this moment was immense. This was the first time in 2,470 years (to the month) that Mesopotamia gained independent rule. From the conquest of Babylon by Cyrus in October 539 BCE, Mesopotamia had been reduced to a client state or province for numerous successive empires and powers. Following the fall of Persepolis to Alexander the Great, Mesopotamia became Hellenic; it was subsequently fought over by the Seleucids, the Romans, the Parthians, the Byzantines and Sassanids, the Muslims and Mongols, until eventually coming under the rule of the Ottomans. When the Ottomans fell in the 1920s, the British held sway over the Mesopotamians. Come 1932, they were, at long last, free.

It seems fitting that Mesopotamia gain its independence again at this time. The fall of Babylon to Cyrus represented the transition from the ancient era to the modern, from the age of the Near East to that defined by Hellenism, Roman expansionism, Islam and Christianity, the west and the east. It is the era we live in to this day, but it is also an era that is slowly drawing to a close.

From the founding of Eridu in the sixth millennium BCE to the fall of Babylon in the first, the story of Mesopotamia spans almost 5,000 years—double the time that has passed since its fall. It is a length of time that is almost impossible to comprehend, especially in a world that is advancing exponentially. But the same changes we see in Mesopotamians near the end of their era are rearing their heads in our own time—a profound uncertainty about the future, a growing obsession with the past, and the dramatic development of a new culture and language—a digital revolution, an entirely new way of looking at the world that far surpasses the cultural changes following the introduction of the Aramaic alphabet during the Assyrian period.

As such, the lessons of the past have never been more relevant. Despite the yawning chasm of time between their time and our own, there are certain things about human psychology that have not changed, and our responses to change will surely be similar to those of our ancestors, two and a half millennia ago. As we look back at the past from a great distance, we can see its sweeping patterns, the paths, and connections that one could never hope to see when immersed in their own time.

From nomadic groups and agricultural communities dotted along the banks of the Tigris and the Euphrates, a culture and civilization as yet unsurpassed emerged. The advances they made, from simple baked-brick cities to towering ziggurats; from flimsy, local theocracies to semi-totalitarian communist states and sweeping military empires; from simple, recited tales to sweeping epics and great myths which explored the nature of the world, the place of humans in it, and laid the foundation for the Greeks and Romans that followed; technology, law, education, mathematics, science; the Mesopotamians laid the foundation for the entirety of human civilization as we know it today. Without the contributions of the Sumerians, Akkadians, Babylonians, and Assyrians, we would never have reached the heights we have. We owe everything to that civilization, many thousands of years ago.

They were a civilization of immense creativity, innovation, and longevity. Empires rose and fell, cities were reduced to rubble, but the culture itself continued, inherited by locals and newcomers alike, each carrying the torch for future generations. When disaster struck, the Mesopotamians returned to their smaller cities and clung to their culture as if their lives depended upon it. When they found glory, they spread their beliefs and knowledge across the known world, with a reach and influence beyond any contemporary. They were a truly multicultural society, providing a template, and perhaps a lesson, to those of us today who are divided by ethnic, social, and national differences. Without the interaction and co-operation of so many ethnicities and backgrounds, their civilization could never have flourished as it did.

It was, from one perspective, not only the earliest but also the greatest civilization in history. It is an immeasurable tragedy that the stories, the history, the names of great *Lugal* and emperors, are known by so few today. The culture of Mesopotamia is not one we can afford to lose, and its memory is important now more than ever before. History repeats itself, forming great, arcing patterns imprinted across the canvas of time, and we still have so much more to learn from the ancient past. As we piece together their stories, and as we come to understand their principles, practices, and beliefs, we can slowly but surely bring history to life.

Free Bonus from HBA: Ebook Bundle

Greetings!

First of all, thank you for reading our books. As fellow passionate readers of history and mythology we aim to create the very best books for our readers.

Now, we invite you to join our VIP list. As a welcome gift we offer the History & Mythology Ebook Bundle below for free. Plus you can be the first to receive new books and exclusives! Remember it's 100% free to join.

Simply follow the link below to join.

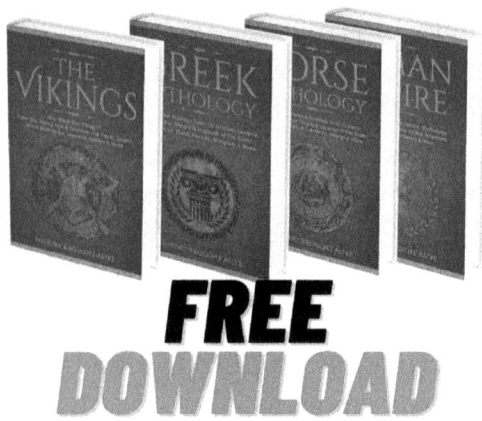

(https://www.subscribepage.com/hba)

Keep upto date with us on:

YouTube: History Brought Alive

Facebook: History Brought Alive

www.historybroughtalive.com

References

Avery, J. S. (2016). *Science and society*. World Scientific.

Carroll, R. P., & Prickett, S. (2008). *The Bible: Authorized King James version*. Oxford University Press.

Gadd, C. J. (1977). Assyria and Babylon c. 1370-1300 B.C. In Edwards, I. E. S., Gadd, C. J., & Hammond, N. G. L. (Ed.), *The Cambridge Ancient History, Volumes 2 Part 2: The Middle East and the Aegean Region c. 1380-1000 B.C.*(3rd ed., pp. 21-48). Cambridge University Press.

Herodotus. (2015). *The histories*. (T. Holland, Trans.). Penguin Books.

Hirth, K. (2020). The organization of ancient economies: A global perspective. Cambridge University Press

Kramer, S. N. (1971). *The Sumerians*. University of Chicago Press.

Kriwaczek, P. (2010). Babylon: Mesopotamia and the birth of civilization. Thomas Dunne Books.

Lerner, G. (1986). The origin of prostitution in Ancient Mesopotamia. *Signs, 11*(2), 236-254. https://www.jstor.org/stable/3174047

Livius.org. (2020, September 24). *The Sumerian king list.* Livius.org. https://www.livius.org/sources/content/anet/266-the-sumerian-king-list/

Mark, J. J. (2014, July 9). *Ashurnasirpal II.* World History Encyclopedia. https://www.worldhistory.org/Ashurnasirpal_II/

Richardson, M. E. J. (2000). *Hammurabi's laws: Text, translation and glossary.* T&T Clark International.

Spar, I. (1988). Cuneiform texts in the Metropolitan Museum of Art volume I: Tablets, cones, and bricks of the third and second millennia B.C. The Metropolitan Museum of Art.

Vlaardingerbroek, M. (2004). The founding of Nineveh and Babylon in Greek historiography. *Iraq, 66,* 233–241. https://doi.org/10.1017/s0021088900001819